THE BEDFORD SERIES IN HISTORY AND CULTURE

Napoleon:
Symbol for an Age

A Brief History with Documents

Related Titles in
THE BEDFORD SERIES IN HISTORY AND CULTURE
Advisory Editors: Lynn Hunt, *University of California, Los Angeles*
David W. Blight, *Yale University*
Bonnie G. Smith, *Rutgers University*
Natalie Zemon Davis, *Princeton University*
Ernest R. May, *Harvard University*

Louis XIV and Absolutism: A Brief Study with Documents
William Beik, *Emory University*

The Enlightenment: A Brief History with Documents
Margaret C. Jacob, *University of California, Los Angeles*

CANDIDE *by Voltaire*
Translated, Edited, and with an Introduction by Daniel Gordon, *University of Massachusetts Amherst*

The French Revolution and Human Rights: A Brief Documentary History
Edited, Translated, and with an Introduction by Lynn Hunt, *University of California, Los Angeles*

Slave Revolution in the Caribbean, 1789–1804: A Brief History with Documents
Laurent Dubois, *Michigan State University*, and John D. Garrigus, *Jacksonville University*

European Romanticism: A Brief History with Documents
Warren Breckman, *University of Pennsylvania*

ON LIBERTY *by John Stuart Mill: With Related Documents*
Edited with an Introduction by Alan Kahan

France and the Dreyfus Affair: A Documentary History
Michael Burns, *Mount Holyoke College*

Charles de Gaulle: A Brief Biography with Documents
Charles G. Cogan, *Harvard University*

Pioneers of European Integration and Peace, 1945–1963: A Brief History with Documents
Sherrill Brown Wells, *George Washington University*

THE BEDFORD SERIES IN HISTORY AND CULTURE

Napoleon:
Symbol for an Age
A Brief History with Documents

Rafe Blaufarb

Florida State University

BEDFORD/ST. MARTIN'S   Boston ♦ New York

For Bedford/St. Martin's

Publisher for History: Mary V. Dougherty
Director of Development for History: Jane Knetzger
Developmental Editor: Arthur Johnson
Editorial Assistant: Laurel Damashek
Senior Production Supervisor: Dennis J. Conroy
Production Associate: Sarah Ulicny
Executive Marketing Manager: Jenna Bookin Barry
Project Management: Books By Design, Inc.
Index: Books By Design, Inc.
Text Design: Claire Seng-Niemoeller
Cover Design: Liz Tardiff
Cover Art: *Le General Bonaparte à Arcole, November 17, 1796,* by Antoine Jean Gros
    (1771–1835), late 1796, early 1797. Oil on canvas, 134 × 104 cm. Photo: Erich
    Lessing/Art Resource, N.Y.
Composition: Stratford/TexTech
Printing and Binding: RR Donnelley & Sons Company

President: Joan E. Feinberg
Editorial Director: Denise B. Wydra
Director of Marketing: Karen Melton Soeltz
Director of Editing, Design, and Production: Marcia Cohen
Manager, Publishing Services: Emily Berleth

Library of Congress Control Number: 2007925240

For information, write: Bedford/St. Martin's, 75 Arlington Street, Boston, MA 02116
(617-399-4000)

ISBN-10: 0-312-43110-4
ISBN-13: 978-0-312-43110-5

Acknowledgments

Acknowledgments and copyrights are continued at the back of the book on
page 222, which constitutes a continuation of the copyright page.

Foreword

The Bedford Series in History and Culture is designed so that readers can study the past as historians do.

The historian's first task is finding the evidence. Documents, letters, memoirs, interviews, pictures, movies, novels, or poems can provide facts and clues. Then the historian questions and compares the sources. There is more to do than in a courtroom, for hearsay evidence is welcome, and the historian is usually looking for answers beyond act and motive. Different views of an event may be as important as a single verdict. How a story is told may yield as much information as what it says.

Along the way the historian seeks help from other historians and perhaps from specialists in other disciplines. Finally, it is time to write, to decide on an interpretation and how to arrange the evidence for readers.

Each book in this series contains an important historical document or group of documents, each document a witness from the past and open to interpretation in different ways. The documents are combined with some element of historical narrative—an introduction or a biographical essay, for example—that provides students with an analysis of the primary source material and important background information about the world in which it was produced.

Each book in the series focuses on a specific topic within a specific historical period. Each provides a basis for lively thought and discussion about several aspects of the topic and the historian's role. Each is short enough (and inexpensive enough) to be a reasonable one-week assignment in a college course. Whether as classroom or personal reading, each book in the series provides firsthand experience of the challenge—and fun—of discovering, recreating, and interpreting the past.

Lynn Hunt
David W. Blight
Bonnie G. Smith
Natalie Zemon Davis
Ernest R. May

Preface

Napoleon's life and exploits are richly documented and continue to fascinate a broad public. But the historical context in which he operated and his aims, ideas, methods, and impact are less well known. Students may have encountered Napoleon in the guise of a hero, or possibly a villain, but in either case as an individual who towered above his world and mastered it through superior will and genius. Without seeking to diminish his stature, this book seeks to situate Napoleon within his time. It starts from the premise that Napoleon's personal experience embodied central tensions of the revolutionary era: equality of opportunity and elitism, authoritarianism and popular government, hatred of kings and the creation of new dynasties, civil equality and imperialism, legal uniformity and exploitation, faceless bureaucracies and cults of personality, total war and national liberation. This book looks beyond Napoleon's military feats to emphasize these aspects of his career. He laid the foundations of modern France by calming revolutionary turbulence, preserving the fundamental gains of 1789, and establishing a new administrative framework. On the European stage, his legacy of war, civil rights, exploitation, and national awakening recast aspirations and reshaped identities across the continent. And in the Atlantic world, Napoleon destroyed the old colonial order, ushered in a century of British hegemony, and helped plant the seeds of American power. Above all, by outshining his crowned contemporaries of illustrious lineage, Napoleon discredited traditional notions of hereditary superiority and dealt a heavy blow to the old order.

This book begins with an introduction framing the key issues of Napoleon's life and times. It takes the form of a narrative, punctuated at key points, such as Napoleon's creation of the empire and his invasion of Russia, with paragraphs setting out the crucial historical questions, such as the meaning of Napoleon's revival of hereditary social distinctions and the extent of his military ambitions, that these events raise. The introduction is followed by a collection of documents, organized into nine chronological/thematic chapters. Brief headnotes situate each document historically. Primarily French, Italian, German, Spanish, and Russian texts, most of which appear here in English translation for the first time, the documents include confidential memoranda and correspondence, police reports, speeches, newspaper articles, memoirs, diaries, letters, poetry, songs, and paintings.

The documents address historical problems raised by Napoleon's pursuit, exercise, and loss of power. Those on his revolutionary rise highlight issues of civil-military relations in the Republic. Those on his exercise of power examine the combination of repressive and conciliatory strategies he employed to govern France and Europe. Further documents on Napoleon's construction of a new sociopolitical order raise questions about the regime: To what extent was it a patriarchy, a class society, a police state, a monarchy, a meritocracy? War also receives the attention it demands. But instead of focusing on battles, the documents emphasize its impact on civilians, social structure, and political life. Other documents on Napoleon's European record furnish evidence of contrasting policies—abolition of feudalism, religious toleration, dismantling of old oligarchies versus rule through fear, economic exploitation, and military repression—that students can use to debate Napoleon's legacy. The documents on his Atlantic impact go beyond the Haitian expedition to explore as well Napoleon's role in Latin American independence and the rise of Anglo-American global hegemony. The documents on the end of the Napoleonic regime and its symbolic resonance after 1815 treat the development of nineteenth-century European political culture and the politics of memory. Throughout, the documents offer contrasting views intended to stimulate discussion and offer the raw material for students to form their own interpretations of Napoleon and his historical significance. The documents are followed by a chronology of major events, a list of questions for consideration, a bibliography, and an index.

A NOTE ABOUT THE TEXT

My translations are intended to preserve the flavor of the original texts while making them as accessible as possible for contemporary readers. Wherever possible I have tried to use English equivalents for technical or outdated terms. For example, the term *biens nationaux* (the ecclesiastical and emigré properties confiscated by the French revolutionary regime) has been translated as "national properties." In addition, when providing dates, I have used the Gregorian calendar, rather than the Republican calendar introduced in September 1792, except in cases of key events such as the Vendémiaire uprising or the coup of 18 Brumaire, which are still referred to using dates from the revolutionary calendar. In several cases, foreign-language terms have defied my best attempts at translation. For example, the morning and evening ceremonies held by French monarchs in their bedchambers, the *levées* and *couchers*, have no English equivalent. In such cases, I have left the original term in the text and provided a succinct definition in a footnote.

ACKNOWLEDGMENTS

I am grateful to Suzanne Desan and Lynn Hunt for supporting this project and to the exacting editors at Bedford/St. Martin's for their keen-eyed oversight. I thank especially Mary Dougherty, Shannon Hunt, Arthur Johnson, Jane Knetzger, Katherine Meisenheimer, Laurel Damashek, Emily Berleth, and Sandy Schechter. Thanks as well to the panel of outside readers for their positive feedback and constructive suggestions. They include David Bell, Johns Hopkins University; Gregory Brown, University of Nevada–Las Vegas; Anthony Crubaugh, Illinois State University; Denise Davidson, Georgia State University; Hugh Dubrulle, St. Anselm College; Edward Hanlon, John Jay College; and John Horgan, Concordia University Wisconsin. Friends and colleagues have contributed to this work in various ways. David A. Bell, Howard Brown, Denise Davidson, Laurent Dubois, Hugh Dubrulle, and John Garrigus generously suggested and furnished documents. Marie Francois and Giovanna Sommerfield helped translate some of the Spanish and Italian documents, and Samia Spencer helped me with some particularly obscure French expressions. Finally, I thank my wife, Claudia Liebeskind. In addition to translating all the German documents, Claudia read and critiqued multiple drafts of the manuscript. Unless otherwise noted, all translations are my own.

Rafe Blaufarb

Contents

The Specter of Napoleon in the Atlantic World

Popular Bonapartism

Return of the Ashes

Last Words

APPENDIXES

Index

THE BEDFORD SERIES IN HISTORY AND CULTURE

Napoleon:
Symbol for an Age

A Brief History with Documents

PART ONE

Introduction

Napoleon: The Man in His Times

Napoleon Bonaparte was one of those rare individuals who so dominated his age that his name is still used to describe it. More than any other figure, he incarnated what many consider the principal transformation of the revolutionary era: the emancipation of individual talent from the shackles of pedigree. The second son of a provincial noble family of Corsica, he navigated the treacherous waters of the French Revolution to rise to command its armies and, in 1799, to become head of state. Ending instability while preserving fundamental revolutionary gains, he laid the foundations of modern France. Over the next fifteen years, he led the nation on a career of conquest that laid low old monarchies, transformed the map of Europe, and made him master of the largest empire the continent had seen since Roman times. Although Napoleonic imperium proved ephemeral, its legacy of war, modernizing reforms, economic exploitation, and national awakening recast aspirations and reshaped identities across Europe. And in the Western Hemisphere, Napoleon was instrumental in destroying Spain's venerable colonial empire and clearing the way for a new Atlantic order. But even this was not enough for his ambition. To make his rule eternal, Napoleon founded an imperial dynasty and a new nobility to serve it. Paradoxically, it was by making himself a monarch more brilliant than his crowned contemporaries of established lineage that Napoleon dealt his most deadly blow to the Old Regime. By conclusively demonstrating that individual will and genius could rise to the greatest heights, he fully realized the promise of the

Revolution, discredited the traditional notions of hereditary superiority underpinning the old order, and ushered in a new age of romantic individualism.

By contemporary accounts, Napoleon was an extraordinary figure. In recalling their encounters with him, few who met him failed to emphasize some trait—whether his piercing gaze, seemingly limitless energy, spartan habits, ability to perform multiple tasks simultaneously, or instant grasp of matters alien to his expertise—that signaled to them his command of self and other. Both during his reign and after, Napoleon cultivated the sense that he could dominate all around him, control events, and even shape the course of history. The aura of mastery in which he cloaked himself was an essential basis of his political legitimacy, but it obscures other aspects of his personal and political life. Far from standing above his age, Napoleon swam with its main currents. Brilliant but not an original thinker, he drew on the pool of ideas common to his culture and combined them in new ways. Whenever possible, he retained existing institutions; when it was not, he consulted the past for guidance in building new ones. A tireless worker and hands-on ruler, Napoleon nonetheless relied on a talented group of collaborators to analyze problems, draft laws, and oversee their execution. Finally, he was acutely aware of posterity and saw himself not as an isolated individual but rather as the head of a family, the founder of a dynastic order intended to outlive him. Napoleon may have been the point around which his political system orbited, but his ambition, means, and vision extended far beyond his own person. In approaching Napoleon, we should try to strike a balance between the man and his world, the individual and his culture, the ruler and his collaborators. Napoleon was not a man out of time but a man *of* his time whose extraordinary career reflected and shaped his age.

THE RISE OF NAPOLEON

Little in Napoleon's background hinted at his future greatness. He was born to a large family on the island of Corsica in 1769, just one year after the French had conquered the island. In addition to his elder brother, Joseph, he had six younger siblings: Lucien, Elisa, Louis, Pauline, Caroline, and Jérôme. His father, Carlo Buonaparte, was a member of the island's modest nobility. His mother, Letitia Ramolino, came from similar circumstances. Shortly before Napoleon's birth, Carlo fought under the Corsican patriot Pascuale Paoli against the

French occupation forces. The Corsicans were defeated in 1769, forcing Carlo and Letitia (then pregnant with Napoleon) to escape over the island's hills to safety. Carlo reconciled himself to Corsica's new rulers and befriended the French military governor. Carlo was rewarded with confirmation of his noble title, a seat in the provincial assembly, and scholarships for his children at French schools. It was thus that the nine-year-old Napoleon and his brother Joseph sailed for France in December 1778.

Napoleon spent the next seven years in French military schools. Teased by his aristocratic schoolmates for his foreign accent and name, he found it an alienating experience, but one that introduced him to reserves of inner strength that would serve him well in later years. He sought refuge in books and dreamed of the day when he would help free Corsica from French domination. He was also a diligent and successful student. He especially enjoyed history but was singled out by his teachers for his mathematical ability. For this reason, he was commissioned as an officer in 1785 in the artillery, the most "scientific" branch of the French army.

Despite his abilities, Napoleon had limited prospects for advancement. Although he was noble, his pedigree was not sufficiently illustrious for promotion to high rank. But the French Revolution, which began in 1789, changed all this. First, it declared careers open to talent, paving the way for Napoleon's meteoric rise. This was just one of the liberal reforms enacted by the Constituent Assembly (1789–1791), a body that evolved out of the Estates-General and was charged with drafting a constitution for France. These reforms included the establishment of elected representative government, a written constitution, freedom of expression, trial by jury, and equality of all before the law. The Assembly also proclaimed freedom of conscience and granted citizenship to Protestants and Jews, France's principal religious minorities. In 1794 a more radical, republican assembly, the National Convention (1792–1795), abolished slavery in the French colonies. To symbolize its repudiation of France's monarchical past and its determination to create new order based on liberty and equality, the Convention also introduced a revolutionary calendar in which September 22, 1792, became the first day of Year One of the Republic.

Achieving these gains required abolishing key features of the Old Regime. From 1789 to 1792, the monarchy saw its powers progressively reduced. In June 1791 King Louis XVI and Queen Marie Antoinette tried to flee France but were caught and returned to Paris as virtual prisoners. On August 10, 1792, the monarchy was overthrown and replaced by a republic. Within a year both King Louis XVI and Queen Marie Antoinette were beheaded. The nobility also suffered. In one of its first acts, the Constituent Assembly pronounced the abolition of feudalism, from which many nobles derived revenue and prestige. The Assembly also eliminated the nobility's privileges, including its tax exemptions and professional monopolies. Finally, in June 1790 the Assembly abolished noble status outright. For many nobles this insult, coupled with the royal family's unsuccessful attempt to flee, was the final straw. Beginning in mid-1791, thousands of nobles, including numerous serving officers, left France. Many joined counterrevolutionary emigré armies forming on France's frontiers.

Even more divisive than the Revolution's policies toward the monarchy and nobility was its approach to the church. To solve the state's financial problems, the Constituent Assembly nationalized church property in 1789 and transformed the clergy into salaried government employees. The following year, it ordered the clergy to take a loyalty oath to the Revolution. At least half refused, disrupting Catholic religious life in France and sowing the seeds of sectarian strife. The Revolution's attempt to transform society thus produced losers as well as winners and set the stage for civil war.

The Revolution's enemies struck back. Shocked by the treatment meted out to the French royal family, European kings and princes issued dire warnings. The Legislative Assembly (1791–1792) responded with a declaration of war on April 20, 1792. By summer, an Austro-Prussian army had entered France and was marching toward Paris. Although halted at the Battle of Valmy (September 20, 1792), the invasion generated a climate of hysteria that encouraged political radicalism, contributed to the overthrow of the monarchy on August 10, 1792, and initiated a period of warfare that continued almost unabated until Napoleon's final defeat at Waterloo in 1815. By early 1793, Savoy, Great Britain, Holland, Spain, Russia, Sardinia, and many small German states had joined the anti-French coalition. The Convention, which had come to power after the destruction of the monarchy, prepared to resist them by decreeing nationwide conscription, the levy-in-mass. In the Vendée region of western France, where opposition to the Revolution's religious policies was fierce, the call-up provoked civil war. In other parts of France, resistance to the Convention's authority was also strong. Outlying maritime provinces rose against it in the so-called Federalist Revolt. To maintain its crumbling authority, put down internal rebellion, and defeat the foreign enemies, the Convention formed a Committee of Public Safety under Maximilien Robespierre.

Authorized to use extraordinary means to save France, Robespierre and the committee instituted a Reign of Terror to cow the Revolution's internal and external enemies.

This chaotic situation of civil strife, foreign invasion, and authoritarianism greeted Napoleon when he returned to France in 1793 after a long absence. Between September 1789 and June 1793, he had spent most of his time in Corsica, on leave from the army, where he plunged himself into local politics. But the same climate of fear and factionalism that was poisoning political life in mainland France spread to Corsica. By 1793 the island's population had split into a pro-French faction allied with the Convention and a pro-independence faction that looked to the British for aid. Although Napoleon tried to maintain good relations with both groups, his family's long-standing ties to France and his brother Lucien's friendship with Robespierre's younger brother, Augustin, made his position increasingly uncomfortable. In June 1793 Napoleon and his entire family were expelled from the island.

Upon disembarking in southern France, Napoleon returned to the army. In August 1793 the Mediterranean port city of Toulon, the last Federalist stronghold, hoisted the white flag of royalism and opened its gates to a combined Anglo-Spanish force. A French army surrounded the town. Through the intervention of powerful patrons (Augustin Robespierre, the Corsican deputy Salicetti, and the rising political star Paul Barras), Napoleon obtained command of the army's artillery. He then designed and led a maneuver to force the English fleet to withdraw. It succeeded, winning for the young officer promotion to the rank of general and his first taste of fame. But the coup d'état of 9 Thermidor Year II (July 27, 1794), which unseated Robespierre and ended the Terror, cut short Napoleon's ascent. Because of his family's association with Robespierre and the radical Corsican deputation, Napoleon was arrested and dismissed from active service.

On October 5, 1795, right-wing Parisians revolted against the Thermidorean Convention in what is known as the Vendémiaire rising. Napoleon's old patron, Barras, the man who had engineered Robespierre's overthrow and was now a leading member of the government, remembered the young general and put him in charge of the artillery. Unflinching, Napoleon fired on the rebels, exacting a fearsome toll, and saved the regime (Document 1). Soon thereafter, a new constitution (known as the Constitution of the Year III) went into effect, replacing the Convention with a more moderate republican regime. It featured a legislature with two chambers, the Council of Elders and the Council of 500, and a five-man executive council known as the

Executive Directory or, more commonly, the Directory. The regime instituted by the Constitution of the Year III was generally referred to as the Directory, after its executive branch.

Vendémiaire made Napoleon a star of the Directory. Now known as "General Vendémiaire," he was rewarded for his loyalty with admission to Barras's inner circle. At gatherings hosted by the politician, Napoleon met leading figures of the regime, including some who would later help bring him to power (Document 2). He also met the first true love of his life, Josephine Beauharnais. An alluring woman several years his senior, Josephine inspired in the young general an obsessive passion that was not reciprocated (Document 4). But conscious of her fading looks and with two children from a previous marriage to support, Josephine married the rising star on March 9, 1796.

Two days later, Napoleon departed for southeastern France, where he took command of the French army poised to invade northern Italy, which was then ruled by Austria. The Army of Italy was allotted a diversionary role, drawing Austrian reinforcements into Italy, while France's main armies drove through Germany toward Vienna. But under Napoleon's leadership, the badly outnumbered Army of Italy defeated a series of numerically superior Austrian armies, while the French armies on the Rhine bogged down (Document 3). With the last Austrian relief army defeated and Napoleon crossing the Alps into Austria itself, the Habsburgs sued for peace, signing the Treaty of Campo Formio in October 1797. One of the most brilliant in history, Napoleon's Italian campaign is still studied at West Point.

Napoleon's military feats in Italy seem even more impressive when one considers that defeating the Austrians was just one of several challenges he faced. He also had to administer the occupied Italian territories, which he soon reorganized as nominally independent "sister" republics of France. At the same time, he had to monitor a growing political crisis in France. In the spring of 1797, elections had returned a moderate to counterrevolutionary majority to the legislature. Throughout the summer, tensions rose between the legislature and the Executive Directory, headed by Barras. The Army of Italy issued warnings that it would intervene to save the Republic from counterrevolution. Both sides made plans for a coup d'état, but the Directory struck first on 18 Fructidor Year V (September 4, 1797) with troops under one of Napoleon's generals (Document 5).

After his Italian triumph, Napoleon was placed in charge of a daring enterprise: the conquest of Egypt, gateway to British India. In addition to threatening the British Empire, the Directory hoped to distance the increasingly popular general, whom it saw as a potential political rival. For his part, Napoleon welcomed the new assignment because the perilous expedition to the exotic land held out the promise of unprecedented glory. The expedition set sail in May 1798. Eluding the British fleet, the French first seized Malta and then proceeded to Egypt, where they disembarked on July 1 (Documents 6 and 7). At that time, Eygpt was part of the Ottoman Empire but was actually ruled by Mamelukes, a Caucasian warrior-elite whose archaic weapons and tactics proved no match for the French. In a series of one-sided battles, Napoleon conquered Egypt. But at the Battle of the Nile, the invaders suffered disaster when the British navy, led by Admiral Horatio Nelson, sank the French fleet, trapping Napoleon and his men in Egypt.

Napoleon set about administering the country. In this, he was aided by a group of scientists, archaeologists, artists, and writers he had brought with him and who were organized as the Institute of Egypt. Their activities laid the foundations of modern Egyptology. While encouraging the institute's anthropological and archaeological research, Napoleon also directed it to work on the practical problems of feeding and supplying his army (Document 8). With similar pragmatism, he sought to use traditional Muslim elites as intermediaries through which to rule Egypt. But these efforts frequently foundered on French insensitivity to local culture and mutual misunderstanding and eventually provoked a series of uprisings against the French (Document 9). With the situation deteriorating daily and news from France indicating that the country faced imminent invasion, Napoleon slipped away on a fast vessel, abandoning his doomed army for more promising possibilities in France. On October 19, 1799, he arrived there to a hero's welcome.

NAPOLEON COMES TO POWER

When Napoleon left Egypt, the news from France had been dire. French forces were reeling back toward the frontiers before Austrian, Russian, and British armies. The country's administration and finances were in a state of disarray exacerbated, it was charged, by massive corruption. Resurgent, the political left was calling for emergency measures—forced loans, military levies, and the taking of hostages to enforce these steps—that reminded some of the Terror. By the time Napoleon arrived in France, however, the military situation had improved, and the general sense of crisis was fading.

Nonetheless, moderate and right-wing politicians had been horrified by the left's calls for revolutionary policies. A number of them were plotting to disband the government and enact a new constitution drafted by one of the group's leaders, the abbé Emmanuel Sieyès. Although theirs was to be a bloodless constitutional coup, they needed a man of action to back it. They were still looking for a suitable general when Napoleon arrived in France. Heeding the advice of mutual acquaintances and the call of ambition, he agreed to collaborate.

On 18 Brumaire Year VIII (November 9, 1799), the conspirators put their plan into action. The legislature was transferred from Paris to a nearby town, Saint Cloud, ostensibly to protect it from a left-wing plot. The following day Napoleon urged the legislators to revise the constitution, whose weakness jeopardized the Republic's existence and thus the Revolution's gains. The legislators were troubled by the presence of this imperious military man. Some began to suspect that a coup d'état was afoot, denounced Napoleon, and forced him to retreat to a courtyard filled with his troops. It looked as if the plot were collapsing. But Napoleon's brother Lucien (then serving as the legislature's president) saved the day. Pointing to a cut Napoleon had received in the scuffle, Lucien cried to the soldiers that dagger-wielding legislators had tried to assassinate their general. Thus aroused, the troops charged into the building and cleared out all but a handful of legislators who were in on the plot. The remaining legislators proceeded to abolish the Directory and form a provisional government of three consuls—Napoleon Bonaparte, the abbé Sieyès, and the abbé's friend Roger Ducos—to oversee the drafting of a new constitution.

Although Sieyès was the most celebrated constitution-maker of the time, Napoleon dominated the ensuing discussions. Instead of allowing himself to be overawed by the veteran political theorist and maneuvered into a subordinate position, Napoleon made sure that he would be the supreme authority in the new order (Document 11). After a few weeks' debate, the new constitution was approved. It vested executive power in a three-man consulate effectively controlled by the First Consul—Napoleon Bonaparte. It established three hamstrung legislative bodies—a Tribunate that could debate but neither initiate nor approve legislation, a Legislative Body that could only vote up or down laws presented to it by the executive, and a Senate with vague powers of constitutional review. This deliberate fragmentation of legislative authority ensured that Napoleon, who as First Consul had the exclusive power to propose laws, would rule alone with the aid of a handpicked, technocratic Council of State. To ensure his domination, Napoleon personally appointed the initial membership of the legislature and the Council. Local administration was entrusted to a corps of prefects selected by and responsible to Napoleon. The constitution was approved overwhelmingly by plebiscite (referendum) in early 1800.

Having monopolized power, Napoleon then set about consolidating the new regime both at home and abroad. First, he and the legislators issued proclamations to the French people justifying their seizure of power. Claiming that the gains of the Revolution had been put at risk by government weakness, factionalism, and threats from both political extremes, they portrayed themselves as patriots who had acted not to kill the Republic but to save it (Document 10). Napoleon then turned to the problem of internal disorder, which was undermining confidence in the government, interfering with the economy, and destabilizing national finances (Document 12). Counterrevolutionaries in the Vendée region of western France had again taken up arms against the government, politically tinged brigandage plagued additional areas, and lawlessness was pervasive. Napoleon quickly secured peace with the Vendée rebels by generous concessions, notably promises of religious freedom and exemption from military conscription. He approached the problem of brigandage and lawlessness differently, through a policy of repression. The centerpiece of his efforts to restore law and order was the creation of special tribunals empowered to judge summarily those charged with crimes against public order. As it dispensed with the right to a jury trial and legal representation for the accused, the proposal to create special tribunals provoked serious—but ultimately fruitless—opposition in the Tribunate (Document 13).

Napoleon also sought to neutralize the two principal sources of opposition to the Republic: the emigré nobility and the Catholic church. Noble emigration had begun early in the Revolution but swelled to massive proportions in mid-1791 with the attempted flight of Louis XVI. In retaliation, the French government had confiscated the lands of emigrés and sold them to private buyers. As long as the emigrés remained unreconciled to the Revolution, they posed a threat to the purchasers of these "national properties" and called into question the entire revolutionary property settlement. Napoleon sought to eliminate this source of insecurity by winning over the nobility. Within months of taking power, he offered the emigrés amnesty, provided they accepted the loss of their properties; made informal approaches to them through his political collaborators and family; and deported left-wing activists to signal that he was no radical. Most emigrés soon returned to France and ended their activities against the regime (Documents 16–18).

Napoleon had inherited an even more potent source of opposition: the Catholic church. Although it had initially supported the Revolution, a series of ill-considered measures—particularly the nationalization of ecclesiastical property and the requirement that priests swear a loyalty oath—turned much of the church and many Catholics into counterrevolutionaries. Republican legislators responded with harsh measures against priests who had refused to take the oath, those who conducted secret religious services, and those suspected of preaching counterrevolution. Far from cowing the church, these measures only deepened the fault lines between the Revolution and traditional Catholicism. As long as Catholics remained unreconciled to it, the new order faced the threat of popular counterrevolutionary disorder, and purchasers of confiscated church properties could not rest easy. Upon taking power, Napoleon moved to make peace with the church. In mid-1800 he approached Pope Pius VII for a comprehensive settlement to resolve all existing grievances and outline a mutually acceptable relationship between France and Rome (Document 14). The result, the Concordat, was signed in July 1801. It declared Catholicism the religion of the majority of the French people (although not the official religion of France), confirmed the revolutionary confiscation of church property, allowed the Pope to dismiss the current contingent of prorevolutionary bishops, gave Napoleon the right to nominate new bishops to fill vacant dioceses, and made the clergy salaried employees of the state (Document 15). He would henceforth attempt to use religion to bolster his legitimacy (Document 26).

Napoleon also moved to secure peace abroad. When he took power, France was not threatened by imminent invasion but was still at war with Austria and Britain. He proposed peace to the monarchs of those countries, albeit on terms so stringent as to invite rejection. When the expected refusals duly arrived, Napoleon marched into Italy, where he hoped to repeat his earlier triumphs against the Austrians. After a close-run victory at the Battle of Marengo (June 14, 1800) and another triumph delivered by French armies in Germany in early December, the Austrians sued for peace. The negotiations resulted in the Treaty of Lunéville (February 9, 1801), which recognized French control of Belgium and the Rhineland, extended French influence over northern Italy, and transferred possession of Louisiana from Spain to France.

Napoleon, however, could not strike at Great Britain, whose navy controlled the English Channel and was busy mopping up Napoleon's ephemeral Mediterranean conquests, Malta and Egypt. Nonetheless, diplomatic isolation, war weariness, economic difficulties, and Irish troubles weighed heavily on the British cabinet. In February 1801 it began to negotiate in earnest with Napoleon. A preliminary agreement was reached in October of that year, and a definitive peace settlement, the Treaty of Amiens, was signed on March 25, 1802. It restored to France the colonial possessions Britain had taken during the course of the revolutionary wars and tacitly recognized French preeminence on the European continent. News of peace on such advantageous terms after ten years of war was greeted in France with jubilation and did much to enhance Napoleon's popularity and power. But the peace would soon prove to have been no more than a truce.

THE FOUNDATIONS OF NAPOLEON'S REGIME

During the fourteen months of peace following the signing of the Treaty of Amiens, Napoleon orchestrated a burst of reforming activity that produced some of his most durable accomplishments. The institutions he created—which he called "blocks of granite"—were intended to provide his regime with a stable foundation. Perhaps the most significant of these was the Civil Code, renamed the Code Napoleon in 1807. The Code sought to harmonize the legal traditions of the French past—Roman, customary, and feudal law—with one another, as well as with revolutionary legislation. Napoleon charged a distinguished group of Old Regime jurists with this task. He personally participated in about half of its sessions. The Code confirmed fundamental revolutionary principles such as the inviolability of private property, civil equality, and the abolition of feudalism. It represented a retreat, however, from some of the most egalitarian revolutionary innovations. For example, the Code retained the possibility of divorce but made divorce much more difficult to obtain than during the 1790s, and it severely restricted the rights of women to end their marriages. It confirmed certain dowry and inheritance rights enjoyed by wives and children but limited them in important ways, and it mandated more severe punishment for female than for male adulterers. The Civil Code thus identified the paternalistic family as the fundamental building block of society and sought to solidify it by reinforcing the authority and prerogatives of fathers (Documents 19 and 20). After its promulgation in 1804, the Code was extended to those parts of Europe that fell under Napoleonic domination and later served as a model for legal codes in countries as diverse as Japan, Romania, and Egypt. It remains the basis of French civil law today.

Napoleon also reorganized the French educational system. The principal achievement in this area was the creation of a national network of forty-five secondary schools known as *lycées*, as well as a number of technical schools, such as the military academy at Saint-Cyr. Thousands of scholarships were made available to the sons of administrative, judicial, and military personnel (Documents 21 and 22). The reorganization almost completely neglected primary schooling and education for women. This focus on advanced secondary and technical instruction reflected Napoleon's educational priority: to form an elite to serve the state. Elements of this educational system, notably the *lycées* and technical schools, still exist and have served as models for other countries. West Point, for example, is modeled directly on the French engineering school, the Ecole Polytechnique.

The creation of the Legion of Honor, an honorific order designed to reward loyal state servants and encourage others to follow their example, further reflected Napoleon's aim of forming an elite dedicated to his regime (Document 28). He believed that wealth unaccompanied by other qualifications offered only a precarious basis for his rule because it encouraged greed and made elites too independent. By creating the Legion of Honor, Napoleon sought to reward those who sacrificed their own interests for the common good and to instill in society their selfless ethos of state service. To make the new order palatable to the legislators, the government took great pains to emphasize its egalitarian character. Open to all irrespective of birth or profession, the Legion would reinforce the revolutionary ideal of meritocracy and reinvigorate the ideal of national service. Despite these assurances, the proposal generated fierce opposition in the Tribunate (Document 29). Numerous speakers underlined the Legion's resemblance to a feudal order of chivalry and warned that it risked becoming a hereditary elite. Nonetheless, the majority voted for the proposal, and the Legion of Honor came into existence on May 19, 1802. It has existed ever since, and although Napoleon used it primarily to reward soldiers, it has subsequently been used to recognize civil accomplishment as well.

The Legion of Honor, *lycées*, and even the Civil Code (with its emphasis on property, dowry, and inheritance) were primarily targeted at the middle and upper strata of society. To win over the urban and rural poor, Napoleon relied on propaganda. Napoleonic propaganda employed not only the written word but also paintings, monumental architecture, music, and public ceremonies. Increasingly, the focus of these efforts was Napoleon himself (Documents 23 and 24). Artistic attempts to glorify him mobilized illustrious historical references—notably Caesar, Charlemagne, and even Moses—but also tapped into deep veins of revolutionary egalitarianism by portraying him as the friend of the common soldier (Document 25).

As well as trying to win over the people through propaganda, Napoleon also sought to counter opposition to his rule through police action. Daily reports from police spies informed Napoleon not only of political opinion in the capital but also of such diverse subjects as offenses against sexual morality, the artistic quality of theatrical productions, and labor relations. The police also directed a program of censorship and suppression that ultimately reduced the revolutionary flourishing of journalism to a mere four Parisian newspapers, all under close scrutiny (Document 27). But by modern standards, Napoleonic France was not a totalitarian state. Relatively few individuals were imprisoned for political crimes (and even then with at least a semblance of due process), torture does not seem to have been practiced, and the execution of political opponents was an extremely rare occurrence. The regime, however, almost totally curtailed free speech and tolerated no public opposition.

Peace with Britain meant that French ships could sail freely for the first time in ten years. Napoleon seized this opportunity to launch a program of colonial reconquest and revitalization (Document 58). His principal effort aimed at reasserting French authority over the former sugar colony of Saint-Domingue, which had been wrenched from France's grasp by a massive slave revolt in the 1790s (Documents 59 and 60). The French expeditionary force sent there, however, was soon decimated by combat with the former slaves, who feared reenslavement, and tropical disease (Document 61). The French finally withdrew at the end of 1803, and Saint-Domingue became the independent empire of Haiti. The failure of the expedition to Saint-Domingue, coupled with the renewal of hostilities with Britain in mid-1803, spelled the end of Napoleon's plans for recovering France's former Caribbean empire. He sold Louisiana to the United

States for a mere ten million dollars and readied for war on the European continent (Document 62). His American dream seemed to be at an end.

But a few years later, after his invasion of Spain, Napoleon again turned to America. With the installation of his brother Joseph on the throne of Spain in 1808, Napoleon hoped to convince that country's colonies to recognize their new king. To this end, he dispatched agents to Spanish America. These agents were rebuffed as the Spanish colonies either reaffirmed their loyalty to their former king, Ferdinand VII, or declared independence from Spain (Document 64). By 1810 Napoleon recognized the impossibility of winning over Spanish America and changed his strategy. He now sought to destroy the Spanish empire, whose resources were being used to support the allied war effort against France. He dispatched new agents to the colonies with orders to foment insurrection and encourage the independence movement (Document 63). At the time of his downfall, he was even on the point of formally recognizing Latin American independence—which would have made France the first country to have done so. While due only in part to Napoleon's efforts, Latin American independence would provoke a fundamental geopolitical realignment in the Atlantic world (Documents 65, 80, and 81).

FROM REPUBLIC TO EMPIRE

Although it is not known exactly when Napoleon decided to found a new dynasty, the shift from republic to empire began early in his rule. As First Consul, Napoleon established a court in which chamberlains enforced a quasi-monarchical ceremonialism. In 1802 the legislature rewarded him for his peace-restoring victories by making him Consul-for-Life, a move subsequently validated by plebiscite. Yet this fell short of true kingship, as it lacked provisions for hereditary succession. What tipped the scales in favor of full-blown monarchy was an assassination attempt in early 1804 that nearly took Napoleon's life. Illustrating that stability hung on one man's life, this event convinced all but the most fervent republicans that vesting hereditary authority in Napoleon's line was the best safeguard for the gains of the Revolution. This paradox—that a crown was needed to guarantee the revolutionary legacy—was accompanied by another. By founding his own dynasty, Napoleon did more to undermine the legitimacy of European monarchy than even the most radical revolutionaries of the

1790s. The proposal to make Napoleon a hereditary monarch (with the politically correct title of emperor) was approved almost unanimously by the legislature and massively confirmed by plebiscite (Documents 30 and 31).

Napoleon's elevation to the status of hereditary monarch led to the creation of a hereditary nobility (Document 35). Although he could rely on the loyalty of the Legion of Honor, it provided a poor foundation for a dynasty. While its members incarnated the values of loyalty, valor, and self-sacrifice, its relatively undistinguished social composition and purely personal character made the Legion ill-suited to ensuring the imperial succession. Only an elite bound to the fortunes of the dynasty by the desire to preserve its own hereditary status could do this. A new nobility would further strengthen Napoleonic rule by rallying well-disposed nobles of the Old Regime (Document 36). Integrated into the imperial order, they would lend their prestige to the regime. Diehards who refused to accept the new dynasty would be excluded from the imperial nobility and thus fade from view. Finally, establishing an imperial nobility would garner international legitimacy for the dynasty by providing it with an elite capable of representing it in the established courts of Europe. Like the Legion of Honor, however, imperial titles were to be awarded on the basis of meritorious service to the state, remain open to all regardless of birth, and confer neither privilege nor preferment.

The development of court culture was pursued under the empire. Napoleon oversaw the reintroduction of a rigorous etiquette and a ceremonial regime more formal than that of the Bourbon kings of the Old Regime (Documents 32 and 33). Yet even with hereditary government, nobility, and court life, the imperial edifice still lacked a critical piece. Josephine, now empress, could no longer bear children. Without offspring, hereditary succession was meaningless and possibly dangerous, given the rivalries of Napoleon's siblings and collaborators. Just as the creation of empire led inevitably to hereditary nobility and a court, it also required a son—and hence, a divorce. In December 1809 Napoleon bent to this political imperative and ended his marriage with Josephine. Napoleon wasted no time finding a suitable bride to become his new empress and mother of his children. By the end of January 1810, he had settled on Marie-Louise, daughter of the Austrian emperor, who had been decisively defeated by Napoleon one year earlier (Document 34). The marriage linked the Bonaparte family to one of Europe's most illustrious dynasties and soon provided it with a male heir, known as the king of Rome. The second son of undistinguished Corsican gentry had stormed the fortress of lineage and ascended to the heights of power.

NAPOLEON AND WAR

Although the preceding pages give ample evidence of Napoleon's accomplishments as a statesman, political strategist, and administrator, he is best known for his military exploits. With the renewal of war with Britain in 1803, his brief but fruitful period of peacetime rule ended. For the remaining ten years of his reign, Napoleon would be at war with a shifting coalition of European powers. Although he won brilliant victories, each success drew him further into conflict with the other powers. As their desperation increased and as Napoleon's military commitments expanded, the balance of power began to shift against France. Unable or unwilling to make peace, Napoleon and his enemies inflicted on Europe a decade of total war—a new kind of conflict that, unlike the limited dynastic wars of previous centuries, was seen as a struggle to the death between whole nations and opposing ideologies (Document 37).

From 1805 through 1809, Napoleon undertook a series of campaigns in central Europe that would make him master of the continent and ensure his reputation for military brilliance. With the collapse of the Peace of Amiens, Napoleon prepared to invade Great Britain. He assembled a vast force, the Grand Army, on the Channel coast and collected barges to carry it across. Worried by Napoleon's might, Russia and Austria joined Britain several months later in the Third Coalition. When he learned of this, Napoleon turned the Grand Army against Austria. His swift-marching troops defeated an Austrian force at Ulm (October 20, 1805) in southern Germany before the Russians arrived. The following day, however, the British sank the Franco-Spanish fleet at the Battle of Trafalgar, destroying Napoleon's last hope of invading Britain. The Russians now came against Napoleon. Although outnumbered, the Grand Army defeated a combined Austro-Russian force at the Battle of Austerlitz on December 2, 1805 (Document 39). The French victory induced the Austrians to sue for peace.

Russia, however, kept fighting. It was joined by Prussia the following year, forming the Fourth Coalition. Before the allies could link up, Napoleon attacked. On October 14, 1806, his troops defeated the Prussians at the battles of Jena and Auerstadt. The remnants of Prussia's army, previously regarded as Europe's finest, withdrew into remote fortifications and waited for the Russians. They arrived in December, and Napoleon moved against them. The two armies met at the Battle of Eylau (February 8, 1807), an indecisive bloodbath. Exhausted, both sides prepared for a new clash. It came at the Battle of Friedland (June 14, 1807), where the Grand Army defeated a smaller Russian force. The defeat at Friedland convinced the Russian czar to make peace with Napoleon. On July 7, 1807, they met on a raft in the Tilsit River and signed the treaty that bears its name. The following day, Prussia accepted peace under terms that stripped it of much of its territory.

Napoleon's only remaining enemy was Britain. Although he could not attack it directly, he hoped to destroy its economy by an embargo. With the Berlin Decree (November 1806) and Milan Decrees (November and December 1807), Napoleon sought to organize a European boycott of British goods, the Continental System. The decrees closed European ports to British shipping, vessels sailing from British-controlled ports, and any ships that had obeyed the British counter-boycott of the French economy. With the Treaty of Tilsit, the Russian czar agreed to join the Continental System, and the French invasion of Portugal and Spain in 1807 threatened to seal the continent even more tightly. The blockade hurt important sectors of both the British and European economies (Document 57). Yet its impact was mixed. Smuggling of British goods into Europe (at inflated prices and, hence, profits) was rampant, and certain areas of the European economy benefited from the economic protection afforded by the Continental System (Document 56). Finally, this period of economic conflict had an important impact on the Atlantic world. It not only provoked war between Britain and the United States in 1812 but also saw the extension of British economic influence over Spain's tottering American empire as British merchants excluded from the continent sought new outlets for their goods.

The Austrians viewed Napoleon's iron grip on the continent with alarm. In 1808 a war party assumed power in Vienna, increased the size of the army, and reorganized it along modern lines. During the winter of 1808–1809, Austria moved against Napoleon. He reacted vigorously with an offensive into the Austrian heartland. He captured Vienna (May 13, 1809) but was stopped at the Battle of Aspern-Essling (May 21–22, 1809). After reinforcing his army, he attacked again. This time Napoleon won a victory at the Battle of Wagram (July 5–6, 1809). He then occupied the Austrian emperor's palace and forced him to sign a peace treaty.

Napoleon took great pains to instill a military ethos and a cult of glory in the soldiers he led and in the civilians he ruled. To inspire his troops, he would appear suddenly in their encampments, inquire about their living conditions, chat about home, and praise them for their steadfastness. He would distribute Legion of Honor crosses to his soldiers, sometimes in impromptu gatherings and at other times in solemn ceremonies before the entire army (Document 38). In later years, after the creation of the imperial nobility, he would reward officers with titles and land grants. Napoleonic efforts to foster a military spirit within the civilian population were no less sustained. The press was used—both through censorship of bad military news and through deceptively optimistic press releases, some of which were written by Napoleon himself—to encourage positive public perceptions of the emperor's warlike foreign policy, the French army, and the military life. Army bulletins announcing triumphant battles and feats of bravery were read in the *lycées*, whose quasi-military organization also contributed toward fostering a martial ethos in elite youth. Church bells were rung and prayers were offered to celebrate victories. And, of course, those staples of Napoleonic propaganda—art and architecture—were mobilized to honor the armies, commemorate their deeds, and celebrate the warrior's virtues.

It is difficult to assess the impact of these efforts on civil society. To believe the officer-writer Alfred de Vigny, Napoleonic propaganda formed a generation of young men who hungered for military glory (Document 40). But other contemporary observers, such as the political theorist Benjamin Constant, felt that the constant barrage of disingenuous communiqués and deceptive imagery only served to corrupt the spirit of the nation and make it distrust its leaders (Document 48). In any case, these were the views of social elites. For most people in the empire, the primary point of contact with the military was the practice of conscription (Documents 43–47). The human scale of Napoleonic warfare was unprecedented in European history. Armies were huge, sometimes numbering more than half a million, and casualties were staggering. To recruit his armies and make good his losses, Napoleon demanded tens of thousands of conscripts annually and sometimes more. Conscription was resented because it tore young men away from their families, deprived their families of their labor and earning power, and condemned the men to near-certain death. The practice of replacement, which allowed wealthy conscripts to pay for substitutes to serve in their place, only served to increase popular hostility toward conscription. Resistance was widespread and took many forms: draft evasion, desertion, simulated marriage, faked illness and disability, and even self-mutilation. The Napoleonic state responded with muscular measures, such as collective fines and the billeting of troops in offending villages, that eventually wore down the will to resist. By 1811 the young men of the empire were obeying the increasingly frequent call-ups, albeit with resignation rather than enthusiasm.

NAPOLEON AND EUROPE

From the moment he took power, Napoleon sought to extend French domination over the European continent. By the end of 1810, he ruled a vast, multiethnic empire numbering more than forty-four million inhabitants. Those countries that did not fall directly under his sway were either allied, subjugated, neutral, or under British protection. In pursuing French expansion in Europe, Napoleon took to its logical conclusion a policy first adopted by the Revolution, albeit with the injection of a dynastic element. During the 1790s, France had annexed Belgium and set up subordinate "sister" republics in Holland, Switzerland, and Italy (Map 1). These had been organized along French lines and made to contribute to the French war effort. After 18 Brumaire, Napoleon continued this policy. He annexed Piedmont and the Rhineland, reorganized the Italian sister republics into a new Republic of Italy with himself as president, and increased French influence over Switzerland.

With his coronation as emperor, however, Napoleon's policy toward Europe began to change. While still pursuing expansion, Napoleon now sought to harness it to his dynastic aims. The military victories he won between 1805 and 1809 allowed him to found a series of satellite kingdoms ruled by his brothers and brothers-in-law. The most important of these were Holland (under brother Louis), Westphalia (under brother Jérôme), Naples (first under brother Joseph and then under brother-in-law Joachim Murat), and Spain (under Joseph). Napoleon also created French-dominated buffer states in strategically important areas. The most important were the Confederation of the Rhine, created in central Germany in 1806 to counter Austrian and Prussian influence and, the following year, the Grand Duchy of Warsaw in Poland, as a barrier against Russia. These creations have been seen as precursors of the modern nation-states of Italy, Germany, and Poland. But after 1810 Napoleon reorganized his empire once again,

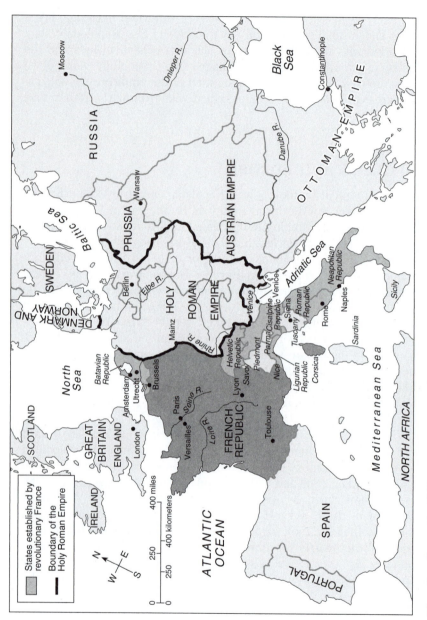

Map 1. *Europe in 1800*

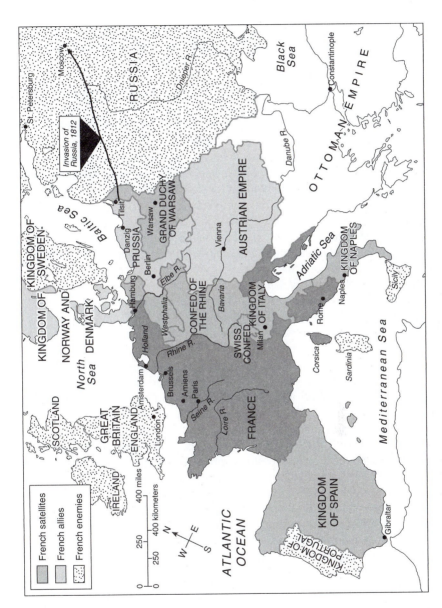

Map 2. *Europe in 1812*

21

annexing directly to France the overly independent kingdom of Holland, parts of Switzerland and Italy, Catalonia, the Hanseatic cities (Hamburg, Lübeck, and Bremen), and some other German territories (Map 2). In the final years of his rule, Napoleon seems to have been in the process of abandoning the pretense of indirect rule in favor of outright annexation.

The impact of Napoleonic rule on Europe has often been characterized as contradictory, as it brought both institutional reforms and heavy exactions. In truth, these facets of Napoleonic rule were two sides of the same coin. Napoleon viewed his European empire as an indispensable source of money and recruits (Document 54). Its contribution was enormous, with the non-French part of the empire ultimately furnishing more than 700,000 troops and paying for half of total military expenditures. These figures do not include the burden of lodging and supplying imperial and enemy armies as they moved back and forth across the continent, nor do they take into account the physical and psychological hardships military occupation and the passage of troops entailed (Documents 42 and 55). The empire served Napoleon's economic interests as well. It supported the Continental System, was organized into a protected market designed to favor French trade, and provided Napoleon with tracts of land with which to reward his faithful servitors. Without the resources of the non-French parts of the empire, it is hard to see how Napoleon could have ever attained the degree of power he did. Naturally, Napoleon supplemented their contributions with heavy indemnities from his opponents.

For the lands of the empire to play their supporting role effectively, Napoleon believed, they had to be restructured along French lines. Only by replacing their old regimes with streamlined laws and institutions could they furnish money and recruits in the quantities Napoleon sought. Paradoxically then, Napoleonic exploitation led to institutional reforms that have generally been characterized as progressive or modernizing. In pursuit of more efficient means of extracting resources from his empire, Napoleon unseated ancient dynasties, destroyed the privileges of church and nobility, abolished feudalism, and swept away internal barriers to economic growth. In their place, he instituted centralized bureaucracy, legal uniformity (often through imposition of the Civil Code), the opening of careers to talent, secularization (which led in many places to the emancipation of the Jews), and secondary education (Documents 50–53). Many of these innovations were appreciated, but two were universally detested: military conscription and more efficient systems of taxation.

The impact of Napoleonic reforms varied across the empire. In general, lands that had already experienced significant reformism before the arrival of the French tended to be more open to their innovations, while more tradition-bound societies experienced less change. Napoleonic reforms seem to have taken root in Holland and Westphalia, for example, while in Naples legal conflicts sparked by the abolition of feudalism were still raging in the twentieth century. On the European-wide scale, however, the Napoleonic presence made a lasting impression: the Holy Roman Empire was dissolved (in 1806), national boundaries were redrawn, political units were consolidated (the number of German states, for example, was reduced from more than 300 to 39), and new entities foreshadowing the nineteenth-century nation-states were created (Document 49).

DECLINE AND FALL

With his marriage to Marie-Louise and the birth of their son, Napoleon's position seemed more secure than ever, his power unequaled, his legitimacy established, his succession ensured. But cracks were beginning to appear in the imperial edifice. Conscription and taxation continued to fuel widespread resentment. Economic difficulties, created in part by the Continental System, exacerbated discontent. And deteriorating relations with the church, which culminated in Napoleon's annexation of Rome and imprisonment of the pope in 1809, aroused the anger of Catholics across Europe. The fundamental problem, however, was that Napoleon was either unwilling or unable to secure a general peace agreement that would ratify the new European order he had built. Enemies he had subdued, such as Prussia and Austria, were not genuinely reconciled to Napoleonic predominance. They burned with resentment at the humiliating treaties Napoleon had imposed on them, treaties that forced them to pay huge indemnities, cede large portions of their territory, and subordinate their economies to French interests. Acutely aware of their weakness, however, they quietly awaited the moment when they could exact revenge. Then there was Great Britain, undaunted and seemingly untouchable. For Napoleon, the island nation remained his greatest enemy, funding subversion against the French empire and, by its mere existence, keeping alive the hopes of those seeking to cast off its yoke. But powerless before the Royal Navy, Napoleon could not strike Britain directly.

Instead, Napoleon sought to defeat Britain economically by means of the continental blockade. But to make it effective, the entire European coastline had to be sealed against British trade. In Napoleon's eyes, Portugal constituted a gaping hole in the blockade. A traditional ally and economic dependent of Britain, Portugal was reluctant to bow to French pressure and cut ties with its great trading partner. Impatient with Portugal's attempts to remain neutral, Napoleon sent an army against it in November 1807. At the same time, he decided to replace Spain's weak Bourbon monarch with his own brother Joseph, then king of Naples. Although the invasion of Portugal was thwarted by British intervention, the occupation of Spain progressed rapidly. By April 1808 most members of the Spanish Bourbon family were prisoners in France, Joseph Bonaparte had been crowned, and most of the country was in French hands. But on May 2, an uprising broke out in Madrid. Although it was mercilessly crushed by the French, violence spread across the country (Document 68). While the Spanish clergy encouraged resistance and the national committee (Junta) that claimed interim authority over Spain in the absence of its legitimate Bourbon rulers called for a war of national liberation, it is not clear how religious or national the struggle really was (Documents 66 and 67). Other factors—provincialism, local enmities, and even opportunistic lawlessness—were also major factors in the Spanish War. In addition, the British in neighboring Portugal gave critical support to the Spanish uprising. Despite the commitment of 300,000 troops, the French were never able to defeat the Spanish guerrillas. The interminable Spanish War was an ulcer that bled away men and resources that would be sorely missed in 1812 when Napoleon decided to close another hole in the continental blockade: Russia.

Since the Treaty of Tilsit, relations between France and Russia had grown increasingly chilly. The czar had resented the creation of the Grand Duchy of Warsaw and Napoleonic opposition to Russian expansion in the Black Sea region. At the end of 1810, the czar withdrew from the Continental System, sought closer ties with Britain, and prepared for war. Napoleon responded by assembling the largest army Europe had ever seen on Russia's frontier. Numbering more than 600,000 men, his Grand Army was composed of soldiers from Germany, Italy, Lithuania, Poland, Portugal, Spain, and Switzerland, as well as France. On the night of June 24–25, 1812, Napoleon's army crossed the Russian frontier. The Russians retreated before the onslaught, drawing the French deeper and deeper into the country (Document 69). The Russian army only stopped to give battle at

Borodino, to the west of Moscow, but was thrown back by the French. On September 14 the French entered Moscow itself, only to see the city go up in flames (Document 70). For one month, Napoleon waited in the burnt-out capital for a peace request from the czar. It never came. With winter approaching and the Cossacks taking a heavy toll on the overextended French supply lines, Napoleon decided to abandon the capital. The French retreat turned into a nightmare. Reluctant allied contingents, notably the Prussians, now switched sides. Harassed by the pursuing enemies and with temperatures dropping sharply, the French forces suffered catastrophic losses. Only a small fraction of Napoleon's once-proud army survived to cross the Beresina River out of Russia (Document 71). By then, however, Napoleon had already left his troops to return hastily to France, where he threw himself into the task of propping up his wavering authority and recruiting a new army to face the expected onslaught from the east.

That Napoleon was able to make up the losses in manpower suffered in Russia testifies to the vigor of the state institutions he had built, especially those involved in conscription. But his conduct in the final campaigns of 1813–1814 reveals yet again his inability to settle for anything less than total victory. Although he rushed his new army into Germany and won initial battles against the Russians and Prussians, he scornfully rejected the mediation of Austria, which hoped to stay out of the conflict by acting as a peace broker. As a result, when Napoleon fought again at the three-day Battle of Leipzig (October 16–19, 1813), his badly outnumbered forces were defeated by the allies, now reinforced by the Austrians and defecting corps of German and Italian satellite troops. Calls for revenge and national liberation were heard in Germany (Documents 72 and 73). These appeals resonated only faintly with the mass of German-speaking peoples, but they nonetheless represented the first stirrings of German nationalism. With Napoleon's army shattered and his empire collapsing, he fled back to France to raise yet another army to defend the homeland. Napoleon performed brilliantly in the campaign of France but could not overcome the allies' crushing superiority. He abdicated on April 6, 1814, and was exiled to the Mediterranean island of Elba, over which he became sovereign. The victorious allies restored the Bourbon dynasty to the throne of France in the person of Louis XVIII, brother of Louis XVI.

The question of how the French viewed their new rulers still inspires politically charged debate (Document 74). On the one hand, Louis XVIII confirmed many of the changes made by the Revolution and Napoleon. He recognized the sale of national properties confiscated from emigrés and the church, accepted the principle of the career open to talent, resisted calls for the reimposition of feudalism, retained most of the Napoleonic bureaucracy (including the army officers), and issued a new constitution, the Charter, which guaranteed a degree of elected, representative government. On the other hand, some of his closest supporters were vengeful, aristocratic emigrés who chafed at their sovereign's moderation. They called for stern measures against those who had served Napoleon and demanded the restoration of the pre-1789 social order, including the annulment of revolutionary property confiscations and the restoration of noble and ecclesiastical privilege. Even Louis XVIII's conciliatory program harbored ambiguities, such as the apparent rejection of the idea of popular sovereignty implicit in his insistence on "giving" the Charter to the nation. Another potential source of discontent with the Bourbons lay in the peace settlement. The allies stripped territorial gains made by the Revolution and Napoleon, ringed France with buffer states as insurance against future aggression, and, perhaps most humiliating of all, imposed on France a new government by force of arms. Whatever the precise degree of discontent with the Bourbons, Napoleon perceived in the situation an opportunity to return to France and regain power. On February 25, 1815, he slipped from Elba with a contingent of loyal retainers and landed in southern France on March 1.

If the question of French opinion of the Bourbon restoration is highly polemical, that of public reaction to Napoleon's return and hundred-day reign is no less so (Documents 75 and 76). News of his landing provoked contrasting reactions. The Vendée, which had been pacified by Napoleon soon after Brumaire, rose against his return. In the south, Catholics took up arms against their Protestant neighbors in a wave of score-settling and preemptive violence. And in Paris, the Bourbon establishment viewed Napoleon's return with horror and dispatched large military forces to intercept him. But these troops deserted to their beloved emperor and thus only served to swell his ranks. By the end of March, the Bourbons had fled, the allies were once again mobilizing, and Napoleon was back in Paris. Former revolutionaries and liberals, who had previously detested his authoritarian regime, now flocked to offer their services. For them, he was the only imaginable alternative to Bourbon monarchy. They hoped that Napoleon had realized that only by tapping into national energies and unleashing pent-up revolutionary forces could France withstand the enemy armies converging on it. Napoleon played to these expectations by accepting some liberal reforms, adopting a more revolutionary ceremonial style, and permitting the formation of armed bands of citizens, the federated volunteers (*fédérés*). Yet in other ways his regime remained unchanged. He continued to rule as emperor and remained wary of popular mobilization—and indeed all political initiatives that did not emanate from himself. Placing his main reliance on the regular army, he devoted the bulk of his efforts during the Hundred Days to readying the army for combat. He declared neither a levy-in-mass, nor that the fatherland was in danger, but prepared to resist the allies by the same means he had always used—conventional warfare waged by professional military forces. Disappointed liberals would blame the fast-approaching defeat on Napoleon's unwillingness to tap the revolutionary spirit of the nation.

On June 18, 1815, an allied force under the Duke of Wellington decisively defeated Napoleon's army near the Belgian village of Waterloo. In the days that followed, the Bourbons were restored by the allied armies that, taking no chances, occupied France for the next three years. After considering flight to the United States, Napoleon handed himself over to the British. His naïve trust in the British reputation for fair play was disappointed when his captors deported him to the remote South Atlantic island of Saint Helena. The former emperor would spend the years until his death in 1821 as a prisoner on the island.

Napoleon's captivity marked the end of one era and the beginning of another. Although Napoleon would no longer exercise power himself, a new political movement would emerge after 1815—Bonapartism. Napoleon played a key role in its elaboration through his efforts to write his own legend (Document 86). In accounts dictated to four loyalists who accompanied him to Saint Helena, Napoleon shaped the way posterity would view his legacy. Bonapartism also thrived on a strong current of nostalgia, as well as anger at the harsh royalist repression known as the White Terror (Document 77). Feeding on popular discontent with the Bourbons and fear of an aristocratic reaction, Bonapartism viewed Napoleon as nothing less than a messiah whose return could alone save France. Carefully monitored by the nervous Bourbon police, expressions of popular Bonapartism varied from full-blown military plots to insults against the Bourbon family, posters, songs, the wearing of Napoleonic insignia, and the trafficking of Napoleonic memorabilia (Documents 78 and 79). Affectionate cries such as "Long Live Little Baldy" and "Long Live the Little Corporal" testify that, in the eyes of the Bonapartist people in France and abroad, Napoleon was one of them (Documents 82 and 83). Even his death in 1821, followed by that of his son in 1832, could not kill the Bonapartist movement. In 1840 the Orleanist July Monarchy (1830–1848) used the return of Napoleon's body from Saint Helena for reburial in France to win political support (Document 85). A decade later, Napoleon's nephew Louis-Napoleon drew on deep currents of Bonapartist feeling to help found a new, second empire (Document 84).

LEGACY

Historians have generally stressed the ambiguity of Napoleon's legacy, contrasting his authoritarian militarism with his modernizing reformism. On the negative side, Napoleon had an insatiable taste for war—resulting in millions of deaths and untold hardship for many more, conquest, exploitation, and loss of liberty—that was matched only by his thirst for domination. Under his rule, the fundamental political freedoms won by the French Revolution were extinguished, and social hierarchy under the domination of a repressive, centralized state was restored. Compared to his regime, even that of the Bourbons—with its pacifist inclinations, Charter, and elected representative assemblies—seemed like a return to liberalism. Yet Napoleon's legacy came to more than simply war, exploitation, and dictatorship. On the positive side, Napoleon was responsible for consolidating some of the fundamental gains of the French Revolution—notably in the areas of civil equality and property law—and exporting them to Europe through the Civil Code. Even his conquests—which led to the consolidation of archaic political units into more streamlined ones with efficient bureaucratic structures—accelerated the process of European modernization. While it is true that Napoleon imposed these reforms to facilitate the exploitation of his empire, the institutions he created were retained by post-Napoleonic rulers. Finally, by laying low so many ancient dynasties and aristocracies and raising himself to the level of Europe's most illustrious ruling families, Napoleon dealt a mortal blow to traditional conceptions of monarchical legitimacy. While the old order would survive into the early years of the twentieth century, Napoleon had signed its death warrant.

Faced with such conflicting evidence, historians have concluded that his rule was a study in paradox, contrast, and self-contradiction. For the leading French Napoleonic scholar, the regime was a fragile compromise, wavering between "a return to the past, a continuation of the present, or a preparation for the future."[1] Another prominent scholar has characterized it as "a contradictory mixture of the ancient and the modern."[2] And, most recently, a leading American historian of Napoleonic Europe has summed up the regime as having a "Janus face."[3] The documents offered in this volume present ample evidence of both its positive and negative features. But rather than remaining content with identifying the apparent contradictions of the Napoleonic record, we should try to discover the underlying intentions and logic that held such seemingly incompatible elements together. Napoleon was many things, but he was not a muddled thinker. It is true that he had to respond to unpredictable, rapidly developing events. It is also true that he used whatever intellectual and institutional raw materials he found at hand to construct his new order. But Napoleon did not act without purpose. Throughout his political career, he defined goals and pursued them through policies that, more often than not, were well suited to achieving his ends. What appear today as internal contradictions were actually the diverse means Napoleon employed to translate his ambitions into reality. By seeking out the unifying logic underneath the apparent contradictions, we can get a sense of how Napoleon understood his world and tried to act upon it.

NOTES

[1] Jean Tulard, *Napoleon: The Myth of the Saviour*, trans. Theresa Waugh (London: Methuen, 1977), 4.

[2] Martyn Lyons, *Napoleon Bonaparte and the Legacy of the French Revolution* (New York: St. Martin's, 1994), 176.

[3] Alexander Grab, *Napoleon and the Transformation of Europe* (London: Palgrave-Macmillan, 2003), 19.

PART TWO

The Documents

1

The Rise of Napoleon

The Making of a Political General

1

JEAN-CHARLES-DOMINIQUE LACRETELLE

Account of the 1795 Vendémiaire Uprising

1875

*Fall 1795 found Napoleon Bonaparte in Paris, subsisting on the half pay
to which an unassigned general was entitled. But on October 5, 1795,
his fortunes changed when he was entrusted with defending the Convention during the uprising of 13 Vendémiaire. This document offers an
eyewitness account. It was written by one of the rebels, royalist Jean-
Charles-Dominique Lacretelle (1766–1855), years after the event—long
after he had rallied to Napoleon's regime and become one of its leading
historians.*

We were not fully aware of the dangers we faced. It was no longer General Menou, but rather the giant of the century, Bonaparte, whom we
had to confront and repel. [Paul] Barras had entrusted the protection

Adolphe-Mathurin de Lescure, *Bibliothèque des Mémoires relatifs à l'Histoire de France
pendant le 18ème siècle: nouvelle série*, vol. 30, *Mémoires sur les journées révolutionnaires
et les coups d'état*, vol. 2 (Paris: Firmin Didot, 1875), 341–43.

of the Convention to him, even though, just a short time before, the Convention had dismissed him with blind and barbarous rigor. Now he was purging a disgrace which had made his proud soul boil for six months; he was rising from indigence and humiliation to command armies and, soon, to a throne. His genius had already become apparent; commanding the artillery at the siege of Toulon, he had ravaged the English in reputedly impregnable forts. In addition, he had another gift at least equal to his genius; nothing could shock or disarm his will.

On 13 Vendémiaire, everyone was armed; the [rebels] had an army of 25,000 National Guards of whom 7,000 to 8,000 were truly determined. . . . Fielding 5,000 regular troops and a battalion of old Jacobins (ex-terrorists, whose sight enraged us), but mainly supported by Bonaparte and his cannon, the Convention calmly allowed itself to be blockaded in its compound. Its troops retreated before us; we held the bridges, the Tuilleries avenues, and the Treasury. . . . At 4:00 PM, the scene changed. A shot, fired from a restaurant by the deputy Dubois-Crancé against the National Guards on the steps of St. Roch Church[,] signaled the attack. Soon, sustained artillery salvoes . . . decimated our grenadiers, who vainly riposted with musket fire. This killed or wounded several cannoneers but others emerged with their pieces onto St. Honoré Street, which was soon emptied of combatants except for those sheltering in St. Roch Church, where they continued their ineffective fire. Help was sought from our headquarters. . . .

I went there with several companions. Our leaders decided to attack the Convention from across the Pont-Neuf and then along the quay to the Pont-Royal, which was occupied by the Convention's troops and batteries. Our heads were full of the exploits of the Vendéen peasants who, armed only with sticks, had often captured the enemy's cannon. General Danican, who thought he had learned the Vendéens' secret while fighting alongside them, offered to lead this expedition; his offer was enthusiastically accepted. We began our march, stirred by the most warlike sentiments, and I had the honor of accompanying the first rank of grenadiers. Our column grew until it formed a mass of 15,000 men; but the latecomers were not the staunchest. . . . General Danican led us along the quays from the Pont-Neuf to the Pont-Royal as if to offer the cannon a better target. A general of an entirely different sort, Bonaparte patiently let us approach. We were dismayed to see Danican and his staff scurry into Beaune Street—a poor imitation of the [Vendéen leaders] who were always out in front. The cannon fired when we were 50 or 60 paces distant;

that was when we should have charged, but our general was not there to give the order or set an example. Yet we held firm and responded with two salvoes upon the Pont-Royal. We had even advanced a bit when, looking back, we saw that the immense quay was now almost empty. . . . We had to retreat into Beaune Street where the cannon could not reach us; but the Convention's victory was sealed. . . .

The Republic thought it had triumphed that day, but only under the protection of a warrior who would soon destroy it.

2

JEAN-BARTHÉLEMY LE COUTEULX DE CANTELEU

Bonaparte in Barras's Salon

1875

General Bonaparte's firmness made him a pillar of the Directorial regime and gained him admittance to the inner circle of Paul Barras, key power broker of the Directory. There he met some of the leading men and women of the regime. These contacts resulted in his appointment as commander of the Army of Italy and a passion for Josephine Beauharnais, one of Barras's intimates. In the following document, Jean-Barthélemy Le Couteulx de Canteleu (1746–1818), a prominent financier, describes his first meeting with the young general at one of Barras's dinner parties.

My first conversation with the Emperor occurred in January 1796. The Directorial government had been established, and I was invited to dine with General Bonaparte at the Director Barras's house. I did not know that the Corsican-born general had studied at the Brienne school and was already an artillery officer in 1789. From his name, I assumed he was Italian, a foreigner who had joined our armies during the Revolution. . . .

Adolphe-Mathurin de Lescure, *Bibliothèque des Mémoires relatifs à l'Histoire de France pendant le 18ème siècle: nouvelle série*, vol. 30, *Mémoires sur les journées révolutionnaires et les coups d'état*, vol. 2 (Paris: Firmin Didot, 1875), 205–9.

Barras had invited many women: Mesdames de Beauharnais, Tallien, and Carvoisin. During the meal, I could distinguish General Bonaparte from the other generals only by the animated conversation he was having with them. At coffee, this conversation became excessively gay; nonetheless, it clearly was of a better tone than the vulgar jocularity that then tended to dominate similar gatherings.

I was preparing to join this group . . . when the general rose from the sofa on which he had been sitting and, addressing me, led me into the salon. There, before the hearth, he said that he had long wanted to speak with me about the republic's finances.

"You were specially involved in finances in the Constituent Assembly," he pursued, "and you have already presented to the Council of Ancients a number of reports in which I see you making genuine efforts to create or procure resources. . . . But you still want to salvage the assignats[1]; stop fooling yourself, we must return to silver."

I was astonished by the audacity of this assertion. Those who remember the fear inspired by the measures against opponents of paper money (some of which were still enforced) will understand my surprise.

I replied that I thought it quite dangerous, almost impossible, to destroy in one blow the only currency circulating in France. [It had] excessively depreciated, I told him, but was nonetheless the sole means of exchange. . . .

"Believe me, it is not assignats," said the general, "which bring to Parisian tables the delicacies that have been served today. . . . This excellent wine was not purchased with assignats. It is not with these scraps of paper that retailers obtain in the *départements*[2] what they resell in Paris. . . ."

"You fear, you say," added the general, "that if the assignats disappear, the people will no longer be able to meet their needs. The people have assignats, it is true, but they know how much they are worth and always demand in exchange for their labor enough to provide for their family. Break these sterile assignat plates. We will survive their destruction since we will still raise wheat, flax, and cattle. The productions of land and labor, agriculture and crafts, will make silver money reappear once there is no more paper money. Have the republic collect taxes only in silver or at the exchange rate of the assignats; permit

[1] *assignats*: Heavily depreciated paper money issued by the Revolution.
[2] *départements*: Administrative divisions of France.

property holders to demand their rents at the same exchange rate and in the same manner."

The ease with which this general expressed himself, his brief and rapid phrases, and the confidence with which he defied public opinion made me realize the type of man I was dealing with.

"Do you think," I asked, "that the new government's authority is sufficient to risk moving from paper to silver without new troubles? Every minute of every day, we are fighting anarchy."

"In France we have silver, cannon, barrels of flour," responded General Bonaparte. "That is what is needed against anarchy; but today the government can obtain neither silver, nor flour, nor cannon with assignats. . . ."

General Bonaparte soon left for Italy, and . . . his many victories, due as much to his political and administrative genius as his great military talents, revealed him to Europe as an extraordinary man.

Forging a Reputation: Bonaparte in Italy

3

NAPOLEON BONAPARTE

Historical, Political, and Military Notes on the Army of Italy
October 23, 1797

Bonaparte's Italian campaign is widely considered an exemplar of generalship. At the time, however, Bonaparte did not trust that his military accomplishments would speak for themselves. He was determined to craft his own legend. The following document, probably written by Bonaparte himself, is an excerpt from the Courrier de l'Armée d'Italie, *the newspaper he published during the campaign. Aimed as much at a civilian as a military audience, this description of the Army of Italy and its general provides an example of how Bonaparte sought to fashion his own image.*

Courrier de l'Armée d'Italie, no. 48, 2 Brumaire VII/23 October 1797, 205–6.

The Army of Italy appeared on the scene. . . . The children of war were naked and unarmed, without bread, guns, clothes, or money. He filled their coffers, arsenals, and magazines by the magic power of his irresistible confidence . . . which produces inexhaustible resources at will. From afar, his name gathered armies, innumerable legions under the flags of liberty and victory. He taught the soldiers to leave behind their baggage. He showed them new tactics and a new way of fighting. They undertook forced marches, swam rivers, crossed bridges under artillery fire, scaled inaccessible rocks, and took formidable redoubts at bayonet point. Small detachments of republicans forced large corps of Austrians to surrender. Each day one or more battles, each a victory. Active and intrepid, the generals served as cannoneers, cavalrymen, grenadiers, and hussars, setting examples and playing with death. With pride, intelligence, devotion and courage, the soldiers served as marksmen, gunners, captains, inspiring one another by their selfless ardor, thirst for glory, and enthusiasm for liberty. This is but a feeble depiction of the sentiments and heroism which nationalized victory in the French camp, which astounded, terrified, and overcame the Imperial forces. . . .

Today, Glory inscribes a new name on her immortal tablets. She has no fear she shall ever have to erase it. The predictions that announced to the young islander his brilliant destiny will be fulfilled. . . . Driven by love of study, which reveals love of glory, entirely occupied with refining the precious talents lavished upon him by nature, he contemplated his future. Calm in his obscure rank, he was full of his future greatness. He knew there are men whose power has no limit other than their will. . . .

The torrent burst its dike, an immense stage opened to noble and virtuous ambition. He emerged from the shadows. He threw himself into the arena like an Olympic athlete, to the applause of the enthusiastic onlookers. He promised to vanquish, and he triumphs. He flies like lightning and strikes like thunder. The rapidity of his movements prevents neither precision nor prudence. He is everywhere, sees everything. Like a shooting star illuminating the clouds, he appears simultaneously on the astonished banks of two distant rivers. Calmness, humanity, and moderation always dictate his conduct and join in his character courage, intrepidity, inflexible severity in maintaining military discipline, and dignity when he speaks or acts in the name of the Republic and its government. He is the envoy of the Grand Nation. . . . In one hand a sword, in the other an olive branch.

4

NAPOLEON BONAPARTE

Letters to Josephine

1796–1797

At one of the soirées hosted by Barras, Napoleon met Josephine de Beauharnais, a prominent member of Directorial high society. Widow of an Old Regime courtier who had been guillotined during the Terror, of noble ancestry herself, and rumored to have been Barras's mistress, the sophisticated woman captivated the young general. Napoleon soon proposed to her, and they were married a few days before he departed to take command of the Army of Italy. Even while winning the victories and forging the reputation that would help propel him to the heights of power, he remained passionately in love—even obsessed—with Josephine. At times, his passion for her even seemed to overshadow his military and political concerns. It definitely burned hotter than Josephine's for him. The following letters from Napoleon to Josephine, written during this period, convey a very different image of the rising general than the one he sought to project publicly.

BONAPARTE TO JOSEPHINE (HEADQUARTERS, VERONA, SEPTEMBER 17, 1796)

I write so often, dear friend, and you so little. You are mean and horrible, very horrible, as horrible as you are flighty; only the present concerns you; a poor husband, a tender lover, must he lose his rights because he is far away, burdened with cares, fatigue, and pain? Without his Josephine, without assurance of her love, what remains on earth for him? What would he do?

The day before yesterday we had a very bloody battle.[1] The enemy suffered heavy losses and was completely beaten. We took from him the suburbs of Mantua.

[1] At Saint-Georges-la-Favorite.

Napoléon: Lettres d'amour à Josephine, ed. Chantal de Tourtier-Bonazzi (Paris: Fayard, 1981), 117–18, 124–25, 139–40.

Farewell adorable Josephine. One of these nights your doors will fly open: jealous, there I will be in your bed. A thousand amorous kisses, everywhere, everywhere.

BONAPARTE TO JOSEPHINE (HEADQUARTERS, VERONA, NOVEMBER 23, 1796)

I don't love you at all anymore; rather, I hate you. You are dishonest, gauche, stupid, and base. You don't write anymore, you don't love your husband; you know the pleasure your letters give him, but you don't write. Six random lines! Madame, what do you do all day? What important affair consumes the time when you could be writing to your good lover? What affection smothers and sidelines the tender and constant love you promised him? Who is this marvelous new lover who absorbs all your instants, tyrannizes your days and prevents you from thinking of your husband? Josephine, watch out: one day I'll knock down your door and be in your bed. . . .

In truth, I'm worried, dear friend, not to have received word from you. Quickly, write me four pages of nice things to fill my heart with sentiment and pleasure.

I hope that before too long I will hold you in my arms and cover you with a million kisses . . . and as we approach the big circle of the sphere . . . , a little kiss well-applied to the little rascal.

A thousand kisses all over you.

BONAPARTE TO JOSEPHINE (HEADQUARTERS, TOLENTINO, FEBRUARY 19, 1797)

Peace with Rome has just been signed. Bologna, Ferraro, the Romagna are ceded to the Republic. The Pope will soon give us thirty million and art objects. . . .

Not a word from you; good God! What have I done? Thinking only of you, loving only Josephine, living only for my wife, enjoying only her, do I deserve to be treated so harshly by her? Dear little capricious one, I beg you, think often of me and write every day. You are sick and don't love me! Do you think my heart is made of marble! Or does my suffering interest you so little! That I can't believe. You to whom nature has given spirit, sweetness, and beauty, you who alone can move and rule my heart, you who knows all too well the absolute empire you exercise over it!

Write me, think of me, and love me.

5

ANDRÉ-FRANÇOIS MIOT DE MELITO

Napoleon and the Fructidor Coup

1858

Even while campaigning in Italy, Bonaparte remained the Directory's leading political general, ready to defend the regime by force if necessary. The need for his special services arose after the elections of spring 1797, which returned an anti-Directorial majority to the legislative councils. The resulting standoff between pro- and anti-Directorial factions was resolved several months later when, on the night of 17–18 Fructidor V (September 3–4, 1797), troops under Bonaparte's subordinate, General Augereau, stormed the legislature and arrested more than fifty of the Directory's most outspoken critics. In his posthumous memoirs, former Napoleonic councilor of state, André-François Miot, comte de Melito (1762–1841), described Bonaparte's involvement in the coup d'état of 18 Fructidor.

The Executive Directory and legislative councils were divided; a numerous but poorly directed party wanted to restore the Bourbons. . . . The opposing party, composed of former members of the Convention and all implicated in revolutionary events, had the advantage of being in perfect agreement over their goal: the violent annihilation of the royalist party. . . . The people, tired of coups d'état and frequent power shifts . . . were not merely neutral, but indifferent. . . . But it was not the same with the armies. Their influence would necessarily ensure the triumph of the party they chose to back. Thus, neither party spared any effort to win their support. The [royalist] party had weaved plots with Pichegru and Moreau, but if these generals . . . had pronounced in their favor, they would have been defying military opinion, then eminently republican. . . .

André-François Miot, comte de Melito, *Mémoires du comte Miot de Melito* (Paris: Michel Levy frères, 1858), 178–91.

It was not the same with Bonaparte and the Army of Italy. The democratic party based its hopes on them, and success was certain if this army and its leader came out in its favor. . . .

Nothing was more contrary to his projects than the return of the Bourbons. It would wreck all the ambitious hopes he would later fulfill. . . .

Once he had decided . . . to support the revolutionary party of the Directory, Bonaparte pursued his resolution with all the vigor and activity of his impetuous character. On the anniversary of July 14, 1789, he celebrated at Milan . . . a military festival. Five divisions of the Army of Italy assembled for this ceremony, and each published addresses full of threats and insults against the . . . monarchical faction. The divisions of Augereau and Masséna used particularly violent expressions: "Does the road to Paris have more obstacles than the Vienna road?" "Tremble! From the Adige to the Rhine and to the Seine, there is just one step." . . .

After this sword rattling, which revealed Bonaparte's intentions and made a profound impression in Paris, he abandoned all pretense [and] . . . held an army corps ready to march upon France. . . . To command it, he dispatched Augereau [to Paris]. . . .

The denouement soon came. 18 Fructidor took place; the monarchical party was crushed, but the Constitution of the Year III also suffered gravely. . . . 18 Brumaire finished it off. On both occasions, Bonaparte was the agent of its destruction. . . .

It was [thus] not the principles of the democratic party that the general had wanted to defend. . . . But obliged to choose between two parties, one of which would have restored the Bourbons and forever doomed his ulterior projects, he opted for the party he felt he could eventually overthrow and establish his own power on its ruins. Perhaps he even felt [on 18 Fructidor] that he had already arrived at this point. But upon closer examination, . . . he concluded that the moment was not yet ripe.

The Politics of Generalship:
The Egyptian Expedition

6

NAPOLEON BONAPARTE

Address to the Army of Egypt
1798

In spring 1798, Bonaparte sought and received command of the expedition assembling to invade Egypt. The flotilla sailed from Toulon on May 19 and, after eluding the British fleet and seizing Malta en route, arrived before Alexandria on July 1. Defeating the archaic armies of the Mameluke rulers of Egypt would prove less of a challenge than administering that country. The proclamation Bonaparte issued to his army before landing reveals the general's awareness of the complexities of this task.

Soldiers! You are undertaking a conquest whose effects on civilization and global commerce are incalculable; you will strike England a hard blow, while awaiting the moment to strike her down forever.

We will make tiring marches and fight many battles; we will succeed in everything; destiny is on our side.

The Mameluke Beys, who exclusively favor English trade, insult our merchants, and tyrannize the poor inhabitants of the Nile, will have ceased to exist within days of our arrival.

The people with whom we will live are Mohammedans; their first article of faith is this: there is no god but God, and Mohammed is his Prophet. Do not contradict them; treat them as you did the Jews and Italians. Respect their muftis and imams as you did the rabbis and bishops; have the same toleration for their Koranic ceremonies and mosques as you did for the convents and synagogues, for the religion of Moses and Jesus Christ.

Louis Reybaud, *Histoire scientifique et militaire de l'expédition française en Egypte*, vol. 3 (Paris: A. J. Denain, 1830–1836), 112–14.

The Roman legions protected all religions.

You will find here customs different from Europe's. You must get used to them.

These people treat women differently than us; but everywhere, the rapist is a monster.

Pillaging only enriches a small number of men; it dishonors us, destroys our resources, and makes enemies of the people whom it is in our interest to befriend.

7

NAPOLEON BONAPARTE

Proclamation to the Egyptians

1798

Bonaparte was keenly aware of how much the Egyptians' attitude would influence the outcome of the expedition. In his proclamation to the Egyptians, the first Arabic-language text ever printed in Arabic, he seeks to win their support.

For too long the Beys ruling Egypt have insulted the French nation and its merchants; it is time to punish them.

For too long, this horde of slaves . . . has tyrannized the most beautiful part of the world; but God, on whom all depends, has ordained the end of their empire.

Peoples of Egypt, they will say that I come to destroy your religion; do not believe it: answer that I come to restore your rights and punish the usurpers, and that I respect God, his Prophet, and the Koran more than the Mamelukes.

Tell them that all men are equal before God; wisdom, virtues, and talents alone differentiate them.

What wisdom, talents, or virtues set the Mamelukes apart? . . .

Louis Reybaud, *Histoire scientifique et militaire de l'expédition française en Egypte*, vol. 3 (Paris: A. J. Denain, 1830–1836), 150–53.

Is there a good field? It belongs to the Mamelukes. Is there a fine slave, a beautiful horse, a grand house? It belongs to the Mamelukes.

If Egypt is their farm, let them show the lease God gave them. But God is just and merciful. . . . The Egyptians should administer themselves; let the wisest, most learned, most virtuous govern, and the people will be happy.

Among you were once great cities, grand canals, and flourishing commerce. What destroyed it all, if not the greed, injustice, and tyranny of the Mamelukes?

Kadis, sheikhs, imams, chorbadjys, tell the people that we are true Muslims. Did we not defeat the Pope, who preached war against Muslims? Did we not destroy the Knights of Malta, fanatics who claim God wants them to wage war against Muslims? Have we not always been faithful friends of the Ottoman Sultan (may God make his reign eternal!) and the enemy of his enemies? Have the Mamelukes, in contrast, not always revolted against the Sultan's authority, which they still refuse to recognize? . . .

The sheikhs, kadis, and imams will keep . . . their positions; each inhabitant will remain at home, and prayers will continue as usual. You will assemble in the mosques to thank God for the destruction of the Mamelukes and proclaim . . . "Glory to the Sultanate, glory to its friend, the French army! Malediction on the Mamelukes, and prosperity to the people of Egypt!"

8

LOUIS DE LAUS DE BOISY

The Institute of Egypt

1799

Bonaparte's Egyptian expedition was one of the first European colonial ventures justified as an attempt to bring civilization to a backward people. To pursue this "civilizing mission," he brought with him a group of prominent French scientists, historians, artists, and writers. Organized

---

Louis de Laus de Boisy, *Bonaparte au Caire* (Paris: Prault, VII), 153–60.

into the Institute of Egypt (modeled on the French Institute in Paris), they would help establish a new model of colonialism. The following summary of its formation and initial meetings, written by Louis de Laus de Boisy, one of its members (1747–18??), was snuck past the British blockade and published in France in 1798.

It was not enough for Bonaparte to have saved the Egyptians from shameful and miserable oppression, and given them a government capable of making them happy. . . . He still needed to establish liberty among them. . . . Bonaparte understood that only letters, sciences, and arts could do this. . . .

He thus created in Egypt an Institute of Sciences and Arts, modeled after the National Institute. . . . It was housed in a very beautiful locale where there will soon be a botanical garden, . . . menagerie, . . . public library, observatory, laboratories for physics and chemistry, a hall of antiquities, etc.

The Institute is divided into four classes: Mathematics, Physics, Political-Economy, Literature and Fine Arts. . . .

Bonaparte proposed the following questions for examination:

1) How can army ovens consume less combustible material?
2) Can hops be replaced in beer-brewing?
3) How can we purify water from the Nile?
4) What is more appropriate, water or windmills?
5) Does Egypt contain the raw materials to make gunpowder?
6) What is the state of the judicial order and education in Turkey?

FIRST MEETING (AUGUST 28, 1798)

Andreossi reads a memoir on making gunpowder in Egypt. Saltpeter is so abundant, it could be exported to France. But sulphur is lacking; we can perhaps make enough lupin coal for our needs. Anyway, Cairo is stocked with gunpowder. . . .

Monge reads a memoir on the mirage, an optical phenomenon which, at sea and in the desert, shows objects suspended in the sky. . . .

Commission named to draw comparative tables of Egyptian and French measures; a second to compile a French-Arabic vocabulary.

SECOND MEETING (SEPTEMBER 2, 1798)

Bertholet reads a memoir on the formation of ammoniac salt in conditions where its existence had never been suspected.

Memoir on the best manner to mill grain; preference for water machines.

Bertholet summarizes his analysis of the gunpowder . . . in the Cairo citadel. It contains only 2.5 ounces of saltpeter per pound. . . .

Monge's memoir on several ancient monuments and the stone used in the Cairo citadel.

THIRD MEETING (SEPTEMBER 7, 1798)

Memoir on a bust of Isis found by Sulkowski on the bank of the Nile.

Memoir of Say on reed, saffron, and corn straw considered as combustibles. . . .

Announcement of building of a windmill by the commission charged with that object.

Memoir of Geoffroi on the ostrich, and proof that it is incapable of flight.

Bonaparte asks the Institute to draft an almanac with French and Egyptian divisions of time.

Fourier reads a memoir on solving algebraic equations. He proposes a method for extracting roots from equations of any degree.

Parseval reads the translation of a fragment of "Jerusalem Delivered."

Desgenettes reads a memoir on illnesses that can be mistaken for plague.

FOURTH MEETING (SEPTEMBER 18, 1798)

Beauchamp presents a city directory that can be printed immediately.

Bertholet first reads a letter of Laplace on the verification of the new measures, and then a memoir on indigo production in Egypt.

Parseval reads a fragment of "Jerusalem Delivered."

Fourier reads a memoir on an irrigation machine.

FIFTH MEETING (SEPTEMBER 27, 1798)

Norry reads a memoir on Pompey's column.

Dolomieu offers observations on the period of its construction.

Savigny reads a memoir on the nymphea plant.

Dutertre proposes the formation of a drawing school. . . .

Costaz reads a memoir on variations in the color of the sea.

Parseval reads a fragment of "Jerusalem Delivered."

SIXTH MEETING (OCTOBER 12, 1798)

Presentation to the Institute of 100 mummified birds.

Presentation of an indigo sample by Porte, a Frenchman long-established in Egypt.

Memoir on eye diseases by Larrest, chief surgeon of the army.

Voyage from Constantinople to Trezibond, and determination of diverse positions on which the engineer Boure was mistaken.

Memoir by Delille on the palm tree of Domm.

Dolomieu's memoir on the advantages of combining the study of ancient geography with geological observation of change over time in the country's soil.

Report on the formation of a drawing school.

Parseval reads his translation of Tasso.

This summarizes the works of the nascent Institute in Egypt. Does it not seem, in reading this description of its proceedings, that France is present in Egypt, and that nothing any longer separates Europe from this part of Africa?

9

ABD AL-RAHMAN AL-JABARTI

The French Occupation of Cairo

1798

Bonaparte's efforts to portray the Egyptian expedition as an attempt to liberate the Egyptians from despotism and backwardness had mixed success. The following document, diary excerpts from historian Abd al-Rahman al-Jabarti (1753–1825/6?), an upper-class resident of Cairo, offers an Egyptian perspective on the expedition.

JULY 4, 1798

On occupying Alexandria, the French printed a proclamation. They sent copies to the places they were going to reassure the population. The copies were entrusted to prisoners the French had freed from

Abd al-Rahman al-Jabarti, *Journal d'un notable du Caire durant l'expédition française, 1798–1801*, trans. Joseph Cuoq (Paris: Albin Michel, 1979), 25–98. In original, dates given according to Muslim calendar.

Malta and whom they had taken into their service. Thus, a group of former prisoners arrived at Bulaq, one or two days before the troops, bringing several examples of the proclamation. Among [the former prisoners] were North Africans; some were spies. They seemed like Maltese infidels. They even knew [that country's] languages.

JULY 26, 1798

Soldiers began to enter the city. . . . They bought everything at inflated prices. This is how the common people became dishonest. Bakers reduced the [size] of their round flat breads [while charging the same price]; some even mixed dust into the flour.

Many people opened shops near the troops' lodgings. There they sold all sorts of food: beignets, cakes, fried fish, meat, roast fowl, etc. The Greeks also opened many shops where they served all sorts of drinks, wine, and coffee; the resident Europeans also opened shops where they served meals and drinks after the custom of their countries. . . .

JULY 28, 1798

The French soldiers searched everywhere for weapons. They even broke into stalls at the arms market. They took everything they found.

Every day, [one saw] camels and donkeys carrying a considerable quantity of furniture, rugs, chests, saddles, etc. Even things that had been hidden or placed in depots were seized. Masons, builders, and servants, who knew the houses of their masters, were requisitioned. In order to gain credit, favor, and consideration [from the French], some offered to reveal the hiding places. . . .

SEPTEMBER 1, 1798

Today, General Bonaparte summoned the sheikhs. When they arrived he approached them with tricolor scarves. . . . He placed one on the shoulders of Sheikh al-Sharqawi, who immediately threw it down. The Sheikh was very upset, his face reddened; he was beside himself. The interpreter intervened: "Honored sheikhs, you are the general's friends. He only wanted to exalt and honor you by this distinction. . . ."

The sheikhs responded: "Even for that, we would not jeopardize the consideration of God and our Muslim brothers."

This incident irritated Bonaparte who, according to the interpreter, declared in his own language: "Sheikh al-Sharqawi is not fit to be president," or something similar.

The other members of the assembly politely asked to be excused from wearing the insignia. Bonaparte told them: "If you cannot wear these scarves, at least place a cockade on your chest." . . . The sheikhs said: "Give us some time to think about it." A period of 12 days was agreed upon. . . .

That day, the population was told to wear the [cockade] as a sign of their submission and attachment [to the French]. Most people refused. Some, however, judged that it had nothing to do with religion, since it was not forbidden by religious law; they thus wore it to avoid possible troubles. . . .

That afternoon, a new announcement was made, exempting the people. The cockade, however, remained obligatory for the leaders and those who had dealings with the French authorities. People put on the cockade when they went to the French and took it off when they left. This lasted for several days. Then, this measure was forgotten when new events, which I will recount, took place.

OCTOBER 20–21, 1798

When this project [to assess the value of real estate in Cairo in order to impose a new property tax] was announced, discontent grew among the population. Some resigned themselves to their destiny. Others began to plot, encouraged by religious leaders. . . .

Many assembled, committed to jihad. Weapons were taken from hiding places. . . .

From that moment, the situation worsened. Agitation grew. The people went out of control, giving themselves over to all kinds of excesses, roughly handling and mistreating people, pillaging, and stealing from whomever they could. The neighborhood of Janwaniyya was attacked; the houses of Syrian and Greek Christians were devastated, as well as those of their Muslim neighbors; . . . women and girls were insulted, the cloth market was sacked. Gangs of looters . . . spent the night pursuing their exactions.

The French stationed themselves on al-Barquiyya hills and in the citadel. They prepared their artillery and stood ready, awaiting their leader's order.

[He] sent the sheikhs a message, but they did not respond. . . . He waited until afternoon. Then, the situation attained its paroxysm. The cannon sounded; shots fell on houses and streets. Their main target was the al-Azhar mosque; it was bombarded along with the surrounding neighborhood. . . .

Everyone fled from the old town, hiding wherever they could. The bombardment continued, . . . shaking and knocking down walls. . . . The noise was deafening.

When the situation reached a critical point, the sheikhs sought out the leader of the French to ask him to end this ordeal. . . .

Once they were in his presence, he reproached them for having delayed coming and accused them of negligence. The sheikhs apologized. The leader of the French accepted their apologies and ordered an end to the bombardment.

NOVEMBER 10, 1798

Today the inhabitants of Birkat al-Azbakiyya and the surrounding area were ordered to leave in order to allow [the French] to group together in that neighborhood and no longer live among Muslims. The situation had gotten to the point where only armed Frenchmen dared go about. In the city, no one went out except for a precise reason. Those without arms procured batons, whips, or other objects.

DECEMBER 24, 1798

Bonaparte's Proclamation:

In the name of God, the Clement and Merciful! From the general of the French troops to all the inhabitants of Egypt, without distinction.

Misled, inexperienced, and irresponsible people have incited the population of Cairo to revolt and dissension. God made them perish for their bad actions and perverse intentions.

The Creator—praised be He—has directed me to act with gentleness and clemency. I have obeyed his order and, toward you, I have been clement and compassionate. . . .

Men of religious learning and birth, inform your people and communities that whoever rises up and opposes me is casting himself into an insane and spiritually-perverse revolt. He will have no hope of salvation, either in my eyes here below or before God. . . . The wise man knows that what we have accomplished, with the aid of divine power, is the supreme will of God.

2

Napoleon in Power

Seizing Power: 18 Brumaire

10

PIERRE-JEAN-GEORGES CABANIS

Address to the French People

November 10, 1799

After 18 Brumaire, Bonaparte sought to consolidate his power. To do this, he had to overcome the rival ambitions of his co-conspirators, lawlessness, and the opposition of important segments of French society. But arguably his greatest hurdle was the apathy of a nation in which revolutionary hopes had gone sour. By 1799 the French had seen so much political upheaval that they had lost faith in politics and politicians. The Brumairians' first challenge was thus to convince the skeptical French public that their coup d'état was different from earlier ones. In the following proclamation to the French people, Pierre-Jean-Georges Cabanis (1757–1808), a noted scientist and a member of the Council of 500, justifies the recent coup.

Project de résolution portant qu'il sera fait une adresse au Peuple Français, présenté au nom d'une commission par Cabanis, député de la Seine, séance du 19 brumaire an 8.

People of France, your liberty, tattered and bleeding from the excesses of revolutionary government, had just found shelter in a constitution that promised repose.[1] ... Your military glory overshadowed the greatest memories of antiquity; in astonished admiration, the peoples of Europe trembled before it and secretly prayed for your success. Your enemies begged for peace; in a word, everything seemed to be coming together to ensure the tranquil enjoyment of liberty and well-being. . . .

But seditious men unrelentingly assaulted . . . your constitution's weak points. . . . Soon, the constitutional regime was a whirlwind of revolutions, which the different parties successively manipulated; even those who sincerely wanted to maintain the constitution constantly had to violate it to prevent its demise. This state of governmental instability produced even greater legislative instability; and the most sacred social rights were at the mercy of the whims of factions and events.

It is time to end these storms; it is time to ensure civic liberty, popular sovereignty, the independence of constitutional powers, and the republic, whose name has served all too often to consecrate the violation of every principle; it is time that the great nation had a government worthy of it, a firm and wise government which can give you a prompt and durable peace and bring you true well-being.

People of France, these are the considerations that motivated the vigorous determinations of the Legislative Body.

A provisional government has been instituted to speed the definitive and complete reorganization of all parts of the public establishment; it has sufficient force to see that laws are respected, to protect peaceful citizens, to crush plotters and evildoers.

Royalism will no longer rear its head; the hideous traces of revolutionary government are effaced; republic and liberty will no longer be empty words; a new era is beginning.

---

[1]This is a reference to the Constitution of the Year III, instituted in 1795, which underpinned the Directorial regime.

11

ANTOINE-CLAIRE THIBAUDEAU

Creation of the Consular Government

1834

The Brumaire coup had originally been conceived as a parliamentary maneuver to overturn the Directorial constitution and replace it with a new one drafted by the abbé Emmanuel-Joseph Sieyès (1748–1836), a leading conspirator. The military was to have played only a supporting role. But Sieyès and his allies had not counted on the force, shrewdness, and ambition of the general they invited to take part in the coup, General Bonaparte. In the following document, Antoine-Claire Thibaudeau (1765–1854), a revolutionary politician who rallied to Napoleon's regime and served it as a prefect for many years, recounts how Bonaparte outmaneuvered Sieyès and made himself master of the new government.

Sieyès saw with secret satisfaction that the time had finally come to give France the organization of which he had long dreamed.... He wanted to deprive the people of direct elections and reduce their role to naming lists of notables.... The initial lists would be composed of all republicans who had been named by the people or government to public functions ... and who thus had a stake in maintaining the principles and results of the revolution. Any citizen who had been a legislator, Director, leading magistrate or administrator, ambassador, general, etc. was automatically placed on the national list....

The system of lists of notables was adopted ... but [Sieyès's] transitional measure on their initial formation was rejected....

Although lacking personal experience, [Bonaparte] was astute enough to perceive in [Sieyès's plan] dispositions which could hinder or temper executive power, which the general was then upholding as his own cause. All changes to Sieyès's plan in favor of this power were thus the work of the general who, as early as 1797, had wanted a legislature *without standing, without eyes, without ears.* ... Bonaparte thus

Antoine-Claire Thibaudeau, *Histoire de la France et de Napoléon Bonaparte de 1799 à 1815*, vol. 1 (Paris: Renouard, 1834), 96–115.

let neither Sieyès nor Daunou[1] have his way. It often transpired that the latter would be raising one hand against a proposition at the same time as he was transcribing it with the other. Bonaparte astonished [the participants] in these discussions by his ease, profundity, and above all the dexterity with which he identified the weakness of his adversaries' opinions.... We were far from expecting that a man of his age, who had lived in camps, would develop such sense and aptitude in [such] matters....

The moment finally came when Sieyès revealed his [plans for] the organization of the government.... He proposed a grand elector... with a revenue of 6 million, a guard of 3,000 men, and Versailles as residence: he would accredit ambassadors.... The acts of government, laws, and justice would be rendered in his name. He would be the sole representative of national glory, power, dignity; he would appoint two consuls, one of war and one of peace.... He could dismiss and change them....

[As] Bonaparte wanted the government for himself, ... this organization displeased him more than all the rest; he fought it vigorously. "If he restricts himself to the functions you give him, the grand elector will be not merely a shadow, but the withered shadow of a do-nothing king. Do you know someone so base as to please himself with such mockery? But if he abuses his prerogative, you give him absolute power. For example, if I were grand elector, I would say to my consuls of war and peace: 'If you appoint a minister or sign an act without my approval, I will dismiss you.'... On the other hand, what will be the situation of these two consuls?... The first will be surrounded by judges, administrators, financiers, and magistrates; the second, by soldiers: one will want money and recruits for his armies; the other will not want to furnish them. Such a government is monstrous, composed of completely unreasonable, incompatible ideas."...

Sieyès's system seemed a bizarre innovation and succumbed less from rational argument than ridicule.... Instead, we simply created, under the name of First Consul, a temporary president of the republic and, so as not to shock republican opinion..., adjoined... two nominal consuls with consultative power only. The most fervent republicans on the commission tried everything to limit or balance the functions of this supreme magistracy; but Bonaparte, to whom it was destined, insisted that it be given all the attributes of royalty and the greatest independence....

[1]The commission's secretary.

We did not wait for the list of notables, prescribed by the constitution, to organize the national authorities. . . . The First Consul appointed the councilors of State and then the senators who chose, under the government's supervision, the members of the Legislative Body and Tribunate. What vast patronage in Bonaparte's hands! What a vast field for rivalries, intrigue, talents, mediocrity!

The authors and supporters of 18 Brumaire were given the first places in these bodies. Few had not taken part in the revolution, but most were known for their monarchical opinions. The Tribunate became the refuge of republicans.

Restoring Order

12

JUDGE CHALLAMEL

Letter on Brigandage

February 13, 1800

When Bonaparte took power, much of France was wracked by lawlessness. The sources of disorder were intertwined — economic hardship, unemployment, draft evasion, counterrevolutionary sentiment, and a weak administrative and judicial apparatus. The following report on brigandage in the remote, mountainous département of the Ardèche, submitted to the minister of justice by a local judge, describes the lawlessness in his district and analyzes its causes.

Crime is increasing frightfully. The penal laws are insufficient to check it. I must tell the government; it alone can remedy the ills which cover this unfortunate land. . . .

Archives de la Guerre, B¹³ 119, Letter of Challamel, director of the jury of the arrondissement of Largentière (24 Pluviôse VIII).

Peaceful citizens, friends of the revolution, and public officials have no security. Many municipal agents and government commissioners have been shot by the brigands. Of four government commissioners appointed to the canton of Largentière since the Constitution of the Year III, two have been killed and the others, wounded by bullets, were lucky to escape with their lives. . . . The only man able to instill fear in the brigands (thanks to his extraordinary courage, tireless activity, and vast local knowledge) has just been killed in the center of Aubenas by seven or eight villains who shot him four times.

The brigands punish civic virtue with death. A thousand good citizens have been massacred, their properties pillaged, ravaged, burned because of their devotion to public good. How many purchasers of national property[1] have not had their throats slit? Most survive only by giving the brigands the revenue from the property they acquired.

Most tax collectors in this area have been robbed, both at home and on the highways. . . . The national treasury of Joyeuse, stolen in the Year VI on the road from La Chapelle to Aubenas and barely saved the following year by fifty courageous soldiers [of the escort] whom the brigands attacked at Lescrinet, has just been stolen from the collector's house and its guards disarmed in the town center. Toward the end of the Year VII, one hundred brigands forcibly freed several of their accomplices from the Aubenas jail. A month ago, they freed from the center of Barjac two of their leaders whom the military court . . . had sent before the criminal court of the Ardèche. Thirty entire villages have been publicly disarmed in broad daylight. Several have been subjected to heavy contributions. . . .

Such is the domination of the brigands here. . . . They are organized, supported, and directed by men who lost their privileges in the revolution and believe that chaos and anarchy will restore what liberty took from them. They enroll in their murderous bands deserters who, too cowardly to join the armies, are bad enough to turn to crime. . . . These gangs are swollen by a crowd of hardened criminals. . . .

Courts are powerless against such disorders. How can they punish a crime when the witnesses refuse to name the criminals? Few witnesses have the courage to tell the entire truth. Their declarations are almost entirely dictated by fear, if not complicity. We see this, above all, when the accused is present at the deposition; then crimes

---

[1] *national property*: Emigré and church property confiscated by the revolutionary government and sold to private buyers.

committed before the eyes of the witnesses have not been seen by
them and the villain ... is described as a man endowed with all virtues.
Brigandage has ensured itself impunity by making its vengeance
feared. . . . Many have died for telling the truth.

13

**ANTOINE-FRANÇOIS DELPIERRE
AND BENJAMIN CONSTANT**

Debate over the Creation
of Special Military Commissions

January 24–25, 1801

*The First Consul responded to the problem of lawlessness by proposing
the formation of special military commissions. Dispensing with jury trial
and legal representation for the accused, the commissions were to have
jurisdiction over a wide range of political crimes, including threats
against purchasers of nationalized church and emigré property. The proposal sparked a fierce debate in the Tribunate in January 1801 between
deputies who believed the measure necessary to restore order and those
who feared that it would undermine civil liberty. Those favoring the creation of the commissions prevailed. The following speeches by Antoine-
François Delpierre (1764–1854) and Benjamin Constant (1767–1830)
indicate the main lines of the debate.*

Delpierre

Trial by jury is one of the finest attributes of free government, or
rather, its necessary companion and natural guardian.

But is this mode of administering criminal justice ... equally appli-

*Opinion de Delpierre jeune (des Vosges), sur le projet de loi relatif à l'établissement d'un
tribunal criminel spécial* (4 Pluviôse IX); *Opinion de Benjamin Constant, sur le projet de
loi concernant l'établissement de tribunaux criminels spéciaux, Tribunat* (5 Pluviôse IX).

cable in all circumstances? Does it effectively repress all types of crime? . . .

In revolution, when parties fight parties, when passions replace ideas and opinions virtues, those in power merely reflect the dominant faction. Even the juries, designated by the victorious party, are usually instruments of its will and vengeance. Under its terrible regards, they lose their independence and impartiality. . . .

Since the revolution, the jury has been effective only in repressing ordinary crimes, such as murder, theft, and arson. . . . But when it has to judge political crimes, its severity weakens or disappears. Two causes ensure that crimes born of partisan fury remain unpunished. The first is the fear the guilty instill in [the jurors]. . . . The second is the frequent conformity of their opinions with those of the accused. . . .

While excellent in tranquil times, the jury has increased the brigandage devastating part of France. . . . To persist in the present system would be to discredit this tutelary institution, to make it the accomplice of crimes it cannot prevent, and make it responsible for the disorders which exploit its august mechanism. I know of no more certain means of discrediting it than making it [the auxiliary] of the villains fighting the republic, for whom it is more of a safeguard than an obstacle. When the storm of factions moves off, when partisan hatred has calmed, when society, purged of the revolutionary crimes that torment it, will only experience isolated and obscure crimes, we will again place ourselves under [the jury's] exclusive guard and entrust it with our civil liberty; but first we must have security, which we cannot obtain . . . through its mediation.

Constant

I feel the disfavor surrounding opponents of this project. . . . It is easy to say that we are siding with brigands, obstructing the restoration of public order and security, and hampering . . . rapid justice against society's enemies. . . .

We all want to see brigandage repressed; most of us, purchasers of national property, want these properties to be scrupulously respected; attached by self-interest to the government instituted by the constitution, we want only to guarantee its constitutional force and stability. . . .

"The tribunal will have jurisdiction over threats, excesses, and violent acts against purchasers of national property because of their acquisitions."

More than anyone else, I demand a constitutional guarantee for ... purchasers of national property; my self-interest would reinforce my duty, if that were necessary, to convince me of the need for this salutary guarantee; but that offered by this article would be illusory because it is vague, arbitrary, and frighteningly broad.

What does it mean by threats? How would they be determined? How could we prevent those who made threats from attributing them to other causes than the national acquisitions of those they threaten? According to the spirit of the time or place, any gesture, words, or writing could appear to one tribunal as a threat and to another as completely frivolous or innocent.

Only public opinion can protect the purchasers of national property. ... If it is warped, this vague formula, which would serve as a pretext for endless denunciations and unjust or frivolous accusations, would offer no guarantee.

I will go further. As an owner of national property myself, I do not want [us] to become a privileged class. Sooner or later privileges turn against their possessors; privileges are the forerunners of proscription.

In a society based on property, all acquisitions must be respected. All are of the same nature. They are based on social guarantee and public faith. To believe that a certain type of property requires particular safeguards is to surround it with immense disfavor. ...

The commission's speaker said that the constitution has general rules and a protective spirit that allow it, for its own conservation, to suspend temporarily its particular rules ... [and] that the maintenance of public order could conceivably be compromised by the constitution itself, if it were too rigid.

This language is not new. If I did not want to avoid troubling parallels ... I could find in almost every session of previous legislatures orators proclaiming it necessary to step outside of the constitution to save it, that the constitution was killing the constitution. ...

Similar reasoning justified the laws against priests and nobles, ... extraordinary laws ostensibly established to preserve the constitution they destroyed from top to bottom.

What happened, colleagues? We never returned to the constitutions we left, and by surrounding them with supposedly protective measures, we never had recourse to the truly protective means they contained.

Religious Settlement

14

PAPAL AGENT GHISLIERI AND POPE PIUS VII

Letters on the Origin of the Concordat
July 10, 1800

*Anger at the Revolution's religious policy was the main source of coun-
terrevolution. It had provoked large-scale armed revolt in western
France and fueled violence in other parts of the country. The First Consul was determined to end these troubles by settling the religious contro-
versy. Soon after taking power, he opened negotiations with the pope. The
following letters — the first from the papal agent Ghislieri to the Austrian
diplomat Johann-Amadeus-Franz de Paul Thugut (1736–1818) and the
second from Pope Pius VII (1742–1823) to Cardinal Martiniana, bishop
of Vercelli — describe Bonaparte's overture and the church's reaction.*

Ghislieri to Thugut (Rome, July 10, 1800)

While passing through Vercelli, on his way from Paris to Milan, Bonaparte informed that city's bishop, Cardinal Martiniana, of his interest
in reestablishing the Catholic religion in France; and when, on returning from Milan to Paris, he again passed through Vercelli, he summoned the Cardinal and, with the eloquence he deployed in Egypt to
convince the inhabitants he was a zealous Muslim, he assumed for the
good Cardinal the role of an apostolic and Roman Catholic. He even
asked His Eminence to write to the Pope: that Bonaparte, First Consul
of the French Republic, strongly desires the reestablishment in
France of the apostolic Roman Catholic religion in all its purity, and
that he will willingly cooperate with the Pope, to whom he promises, if

---

*Documents sur la négociation du Concordat et sur les autres rapports de la France avec le
Saint-Siège en 1800 et 1801*, ed. comte Boulay de la Meurthe, vol. 1 (Paris: Ernest
Ledoux, 1891), 26–29, and 31.

he agrees to this negotiation, to return all of his States. Bonaparte even shared with the Cardinal his ideas on several essential points, saying that although it would be impossible to let the emigré bishops return, . . . he was equally disinclined to protect the interloping constitutional bishops whose fate he would leave to the Pope; and that, while it was impossible to return the bishops' properties, he would assign them, while waiting for new pious bequests to enrich their churches, a pension, to be paid by the nation, of 4–5,000 florins a year. He even added that the question of the bishops was doubtless the most difficult to settle and that, once dealt with, all others would be quickly resolved. . . .

As head of the Church, the Pope felt he had to respond to Bonaparte, even though he did not believe him sincere; and after long reflection, His Holiness decided to respond to Cardinal Martiniana.

Pope to Martiniana (Rome, July 10, 1800)

. . . The announcement you transmit from the First Consul Bonaparte, who aims to settle the ecclesiastical affairs of France and revive the Catholic religion, can only be received with the greatest consolation. . . . We certainly regard the reestablishment in France of that very holy religion, which has blessed this nation for centuries, as a glorious and fortunate decision, as well as a useful one for the entire Catholic world. We thus embrace happily the propitious occasion presented to us; you can thus tell the First Consul that we are willing to begin a negotiation whose goal is so worthy and appropriate to our apostolic ministry, as well as so concordant with the wishes of our heart.

The hints you provide about Bonaparte's ideas on certain issues provide much hope that things can finally be settled. . . . Nonetheless, one cannot deny the difficulties this project necessarily presents and the additional difficulties of its application. But we trust in God's grace and in the assistance He grants His church, so that everything can be happily attained in this pious and religious matter. . . . We will do our utmost to attain this goal, imposed on us by religion and our pastoral duty toward such a great portion of the flock. . . .

Inform the First Consul of our dispositions so that he can, at a later time, explain to you with more precision and detail his intentions regarding the different issues we must face for the desired settlement of ecclesiastical matters and the reestablishment of Catholicism in France. No more is needed at this point except God's blessing for a

work whose goal is His service and glory on earth, and the reconquest of such a large and illustrious part of Christianity. . . .

15

JOSEPH-JÉROME SIMÉON

Speech Presenting the Concordat to the Legislature for Ratification

April 6, 1802

*Begun in mid-1800, the negotiations between the First Consul and the
pope reached a successful conclusion a year later. The resulting agreement was formalized in a treaty, the Concordat. It declared Catholicism
the dominant religion of France, recognized the nationalization and sale
of church properties, and allowed the pope to dismiss revolutionary bishops. The Concordat was approved overwhelmingly by the legislature. The
following document is an excerpt from a speech by Tribune Joseph-Jérome
Siméon (1749–1842) in favor of the Concordat.*

Frightened by the scale and excesses of our revolution, [the nations of
the world] feared for the two essential social bonds: civil authority and
religion. It seemed we had simultaneously overthrown the authority
that restrains even the freest peoples and the regulator, more potent
and universal than law, . . . which not only forbids evil but commands
good; which animates and fortifies morality, lends to its precepts hope
and fear of life to come, and adds heaven's dictates to the often-feeble
voice of conscience. . . .

Since we had to strengthen anarchy-weakened government, give it
simpler and more energetic forms, surround it with the power and lus-
ter appropriate to the supreme magistracy of a great people, bring it
closer to the customs of other nations without losing what is essential

*Rapport fait au nom d'une commission spéciale par le citoyen Siméon, sur le projet de loi
relatif au Concordat, à ses articles organiques, et à ceux des cultes protestantes* (17 Germi-
nal X).

to republican liberty, we also had to return to this other point, common to all civilized nations: religion. . . .

If some are strong enough to do without religion, enlightened enough, virtuous enough to find in themselves the power to overcome self-interest when it clashes with the interest of others or the public interest, do most have this force? . . .

The Constituent Assembly . . . was careful not to extend religious tolerance to the point of indifference. It recognized that, as one of the most ancient and powerful means of governance, religion had to be placed more firmly than before in the hands of government; the influence it gave a foreign power diminished, the credit and temporal authority of the clergy, a distinct order in the state, destroyed. . . .

The Constituent Assembly made only one mistake: . . . the failure to coordinate with the head of the Church. This . . . produced schism instead of reform. This schism planted the seeds of civil war, soon brought to fruition by revolutionary excesses.

It is in our divided cities and families, in the devastated Vendée fields that we must answer those bothered that the government is occupying itself with religion.

What does France want? . . . Liberty of conscience and public worship; to be spared derision because one is Christian, to avoid persecution because one prefers the old church . . . to the new and abstract cult of human reason.

With arms in hand, what did the Vendéens demand? Priests and altars. It is true that evildoers, rebels, and foreigners . . . placed the throne next to the altar. But the Vendée was pacified as soon as we promised to redress their principal grievance. . . .

How can we not applaud a treaty which, at home, restores to morality the powerful sanction it had lost; which calms, consoles, and satisfies the spirit; which, abroad, gives nations a guarantee . . . ; which no longer separates us from other peoples by indifference and disdain for a common bond. . . . It was after the first rumors of the Concordat that the recently-concluded peace overtures[1] were made. Our victories had not sufficed. . . . They made us feared and hated. Moderation, wisdom . . . have obtained our pardon and achieved universal reconciliation. . . .

[The Concordat will provide:]

Public worship that will occupy and attach individuals without en-

---

[1]The Treaty of Lunéville with Austria.

slaving them, and unite those who want to follow it without compelling those who do not.

A church subject to all the regulations that circumstances demand.

Nothing exclusive: the Protestant as free, as protected in his belief as the Catholic.

The name of the republic and its leaders take the place they deserve in temples and public prayer. . . .

The ministers of all denominations subject to the influence of the government, who chooses or approves them, to which they are linked by the most solemn promises, and who holds them in dependence by their salaries.

They renounce their rich and ancient endowment. . . .

No more worries for purchasers of national property, no more concern that riches distract or corrupt the ministers of the church; all-powerful for the good we expect of them, they are utterly powerless to do bad.

Return of the Emigrés

16

MARQUISE DE LA TOUR DU PIN

Return to France

1843–1853 (?)

Another source of potential opposition was the thousands of French citizens who had emigrated during the Revolution and, in some cases, taken up arms against it. Many emigrés were nobles and still exerted influence within France. One of the First Consul's most pressing aims was to reconcile these sorts of people to his regime. He thus relaxed the laws against the emigrés and sought to entice the returnees to accept places in the new order. In the following excerpt from her memoirs, Madame

Marquise de la Tour du Pin, *Journal d'une femme de cinquante ans (1778–1815)*, vol. 2 (Paris: Chapelot, 1913), 211–15.

Henriette-Lucy Dillon, Marquise de la Tour du Pin (1770–1835), an aristocrat emigrée of impeccable pedigree, recalls the new regime's attempts to court her and other returning emigrés.

In Paris, I found that many of my acquaintances had already returned from abroad. All the young men were beginning to turn to the rising sun—Madame Bonaparte—who was living at the Tuileries in apartments that had been entirely re-decorated, as if by the wave of a wand. She already bore herself like a Queen, but a very gracious, amiable and kindly one. Although not outstandingly intelligent, she understood her husband's plan: he was counting on her to win the allegiance of the upper ranks of society. Josephine had, in fact, given him to understand that she herself had belonged in those circles; this was not quite true. . . .

When Madame Bonaparte learned . . . I was back in Paris, she asked me to see her. She longed to be able to boast to the First Consul that she had secured the allegiance of a woman who was still young and very fashionable, and a former member of the royal Household. It would have been a victory indeed, if I may be forgiven for saying so. But I determined to increase the value of my condescension by keeping her waiting a little. Then, one morning, I went . . . to call on her. In the salon I found a group of women and young men, all of whom I knew. Madame Bonaparte approached exclaiming: "Ah, here she is," seated me beside her and paid me a thousand pretty compliments, repeating: "How English she looks," a remark soon to imply the very opposite of praise. . . .

She went on to say that all the emigrés would return, that this delighted her, that there had been enough suffering, that, above all, General Bonaparte wanted to end the ills of the Revolution, and so on. A whole series of reassurances. She also inquired after Monsieur de La Tour du Pin, and said she would like to see him. She was leaving for Malmaison and invited me to visit her there. All in all, she was extremely pleasant and I saw clearly that the First Consul had left her to deal with the feminine side of the Court, trusting her to win it to his cause whenever opportunity arose. It was not a difficult task, for everyone was hastening to gather about the rising star and I know of none beside myself who refused to become a lady-in-waiting to the Empress Josephine.

17

MARQUIS DE BOUTHILLIER

Return from the Emigré Armies

1810

The following excerpt is from the memoirs of Charles-Léon, marquis de Bouthillier-Beaujeu (1743–1818), a noble military officer and former deputy to the National Assembly who had emigrated in 1791 and fought against the revolutionary armies until 1800. He offers a different perspective than that of Madame de la Tour du Pin on the experience of returning to France after ten years of revolution.

[Bonaparte] was already First Consul. It was easy to predict he would not remain so for long. We were not surprised, his reputation had preceded him, and we admired in him the pacifying hero and great man, healer of France, restorer of order and calm....

Bonaparte...had announced a milder policy on the unfortunate exiles. They were returning in great numbers. Some were authorized to do so...but others followed the French armies that protected them. I know many families—husbands, wives, and children—they received among them and to whom they provided coaches, horses, lodging. Finally, others snuck in illegally, profiting from the tolerance the emigrés were beginning to enjoy. I was too well known to return in this way. My wife and children tried repeatedly to get permission for me to return....

Imagine my astonishment and joy upon receiving two letters, one from my daughter who wrote that, backed by General Kellerman whom I once knew, she had succeeded in getting permission for me to return under surveillance.... The other was from my son, who announced that he was [coming to meet me] in Fribourg....

I was asked to show my passport only once, at Nancy. It seemed like traveling [before 1789] except for the free and familiar tone of the

Archives Départementales du Cher, J 2192.

people and a few Jacobin[1] exclamations which might have shocked me had I not expected them. . . .

The day after arriving, my wife, children, and myself visited General Kellerman to offer him the homage of our family. . . . He insisted on taking us to the Minister of General Police, citizen Fouché. . . . He was aware of what I had done during my emigration. . . . He received us not as a minister, but as an amiable man of spirit. But for a moment he assumed a [ministerial] tone and said that . . . he "hoped I would become a good Frenchman." I responded, "all I have done proves I never stopped being one. . . ." At the same time, I promised "not to solicit from him another existence in France than the one he was giving me by tolerating my return to my family."

I kept my word. I have not seen him since. I have seen no other highly placed men, even my former colleagues in the National Assembly. To this day I have not even set eyes on the Emperor.

No memory of the past, no partisan spirit influenced me in my resolution to withdraw from society and its circles. I resolved to forget all differences of opinion that might exist between people I once knew whom I would encounter and myself; or at least to act as if this forgetfulness was real.

[1]The Jacobins were members of a network of radical political clubs influential during the early years of the Revolution.

18

PREFECT OF THE VAUCLUSE

Report on Emigrés

July 4, 1805

In the following report, the prefect of the Vaucluse offers a glowing assessment of the progress made in reconciling the emigrés to the new regime.

Archives Nationales, F⁷ 5797.

Four-fifths [of the emigrés in the Vaucluse] . . . are workers or priests. The former live peaceably. . . . The vast majority of the latter work in the parishes, . . . and I am happy to have only good things to say about them all. Among the workers, there are occasional quarrels, as sometimes happens among this class of people; but these miserable brawls stem more from lack of education than politics. . . .

There is another class of emigré who, in other times and other *départements,* may have given the government umbrage and caused it to adopt measures of rigor and surveillance. . . . I speak of the former nobles. Among them . . . are men of fiery character, of irascible temperament, who have sometimes caused slight disorders in certain communes of my *département.* . . . But these are unconnected to the revolution or its aftermath, and any other man, non-emigré, with the same character would have earned the same reproaches. . . . The mayors have never given an unfavorable report on the political opinion of emigrés under their surveillance, and it is my duty to assure you . . . that all accounts I have received of their conduct show them to be worthy of Imperial benevolence.

I personally know almost all those who inhabit the prefectural seat and principal towns of my prefecture, and I am not afraid to name Messieurs de Forbin, de Galian, de Flechys, de la Valette, de Cambis, Granet la Croix, Valory, Anselme, Lantiamy, Mery, and others. To name them is to name warm friends of the current government, it is to name men whose only memories of what they saw in foreign lands serve to establish, with what they presently see, a comparison entirely advantageous to the glory of the hero who governs us. It is to name grateful and sensitive beings who can only pronounce the Emperor's name with enthusiasm and daily seek to acquit [their debt] to him by setting the example of love and respect that all the French owe him.

. . . When they left their homes, they were fleeing anarchy and only went abroad because of the fear it caused them. Can one imagine that they would not be totally devoted to the astonishing man whose first acts of government [tended] to destroy the enemy who had driven them out and who, by returning them to their families, their friends, their dearest habits, restored to them everything which had escaped the voracious system that preceded the glorious administrations of the First Consul and Emperor?

3
Foundations of Napoleon's Regime

The Civil Code

19

JEAN-ETIENNE-MARIE PORTALIS

Preliminary Discourse on the Civil Code
January 21, 1801

Having secured power, Napoleon proceeded to restructure legal, political, and social institutions. The best known of these initiatives was the drafting of the Civil Code (later renamed the Napoleonic Code), a comprehensive body of civil law that was applied throughout the empire. It clarified a wide range of legal issues—civil rights, marriage and divorce, donation, and inheritance—by codifying haphazard revolutionary legislation and harmonizing the patchwork jurisprudence of the Old Regime, much of which was still in force. Particularly with respect to women and children, however, it restricted some of the rights they had won during the Revolution. A premise of the Civil Code was that family was the indispensable building block of society and the basis of a well-governed state. In a speech presenting the Code to the legislature, its principal author, Jean-Etienne-Marie Portalis (1746–1807), explains how it sets the "government of the family" on a firm footing.

Jean-Etienne-Marie Portalis, "Discours préliminaire sur le projet de Code Civil," in *Écrits et discours juridiques et politiques* (Aix-en-Provence: Presses Universitaires d'Aix-Marseille, 1988), 37–109.

Civil law . . . should regulate the government of the family. We have sought in nature the plan of this government. Marital authority is based on the need to give, in a society of two individuals, preponderance to one, and on the preeminence of the sex granted this advantage. The father's authority is justified by his tenderness, experience, mature capacity for reason, and by the weakness of his children's capacity. This authority is a magistracy which requires a certain latitude, especially in free states. Fathers must be true magistrates wherever the preservation of liberty requires magistrates to be fathers. . . .

[The father] administers and oversees everything . . . ; but the husband's administration should be wise, his surveillance moderate; his influence should consist more in protection than authority; the strongest must defend and uphold the weakest. Unlimited power over women, such as found in certain countries, would offend our national character and the moderation of our laws. We tolerate as grace in the lovely sex indiscretions and frivolities; and without encouraging actions which could disturb order and offend decency, we have rejected all measures incompatible with public liberty.

Children should submit to their father; but he should only heed nature's voice, milder and more tender than all others. His name is a name of love, dignity, and power; and his magistracy, which has been so religiously termed "paternal piety," contains no other severity than what can inspire repentance in a wayward heart. . . .

Man and woman obviously have similarities and differences. What they have in common derives from the species; the differences come from the sex. They would be less likely to unite if they were more alike. Nature made them different to join them.

Difference in their being supposes difference in their respective rights and duties. Spouses work together in marriage for common goals, but not in the same way. They are equal in some things, but incomparable in others.

Force and audacity are man's; timidity and modesty woman's.

Man and woman cannot share the same work, endure the same burdens, nor pursue the same occupations. It is not law, but nature, that determines the destiny of the two sexes.

Woman needs protection because she is weaker; man is freer because he is stronger.

Man's preeminence is dictated by the very constitution of his being, which does not subject him to so many physical cares and which allows him more freedom in the use of his time and exercise of his faculties. This preeminence is the source of the protective power the draft law recognizes in the husband.

Husband and wife obviously must be faithful. . . . But woman's infidelity requires more corruption and has more dangerous effects than man's; moreover, man has always been judged less severely than woman. All nations, enlightened by experience and instinct, agree that, for the good of humanity, the fair sex should also be the most virtuous.

Women would be misunderstanding their true interest if they viewed the apparent severity against them as tyrannical rigor rather than an honorable and useful distinction. Destined by nature for the pleasure of one man and enjoyment of all, they have received from heaven that sweet sensitivity which animates beauty and is so easily dulled by the heart's slightest missteps; this fine and delicate tact which serves them as a sixth sense and is preserved and perfected only by the exercise of virtue; finally, that touching modesty which overcomes all dangers and that they cannot abandon without becoming more vice-ridden than us. It is not in our injustice, but in their natural vocation, that women should seek the source of the more austere duties imposed on them for the greatest advantage and profit of society.

20

COUNCIL OF STATE

Debate over the Civil Code

September 27, 1801

Although permeated by notions of paternal authority, the Civil Code was more than a device for imposing male dominance. The following excerpt from the debate in the Council of State on "the obligations created by marriage" highlights one instance in which paternalism clashed with other imperatives. The article under discussion read: "The spouses con-

Procès-verbaux du conseil d'état contenant la discussion du projet de code civil (années IX et X), vol. 1 (Paris: Imprimerie de la République, XII/1803), 277–83.

tract together, by the sole fact of their marriage, the obligation to nourish, provide for, and raise their children. The child cannot institute legal action against its father and mother for dowry or any other establishment." Despite opposition, the article was ultimately approved.

Jacques Maleville (1741–1824): Under written law, a daughter could sue her father for a dowry. . . .

What would become of daughters if, from caprice or sordid self-interest, a father opposed their marriage? They could get revenge only at the expense of morality and to their family's shame. It is well known that these cases are rare; but it is enough that they exist for there to be a law on them.

Antoine-Jacques-Claude-Joseph Boulay de la Meurthe (1761–1840): The action in question was just under Roman law. There, the father was absolute master . . . of his children; as everything was against them, the law's rigor had to be tempered. . . .

Second Consul, Jean-Jacques-Régis Cambacérès (1753–1824): Respect for the father's status should nonetheless bend to reality. We cannot always place equity on the fathers' side and injustice on the children's; there are sordid and unjust fathers. . . .

François-Denis Tronchet (1726–1806): The authors of the draft of the civil code found two systems established in France. Under written law, a daughter could act against her father to demand a dowry; this jurisprudence limited the extreme scope written law gives paternal power; and this is why a daughter did not possess the same right to act against her mother. Under customary law, on the contrary, it was up to the father to grant a dowry or not.

A choice had to be made between the two systems.

The authors were swayed by the principle that, as much as possible, the law should not upset existing habits; thus, they preferred the rule of customary law, which governs most of France. . . .

Another consideration determined the authors' decision: they felt that fathers were rarely harsh toward their children. . . . We must not arm children against their fathers; the legal action under discussion would become a means of harassing and embarrassing them, and of interfering with their business dealings. Sometimes they will not want to permit an indiscreet marriage; but their consent will be obtained forcibly by making them choose between giving it and having their business exposed publicly. . . .

Maleville: Marriage should be encouraged because it prevents immorality.... [Allowing daughters to sue their fathers for a dowry will] encourage marriage, not weaken paternal authority....

First Consul, Napoleon Bonaparte: It is difficult to see how paternal authority, which is only instituted in the interest of the children, can turn against them. Moreover, it is a constant principle that the father must nourish all of his children. This obligation includes that of contracting a marriage for his daughter since she can only establish herself through marriage, while boys establish themselves in many other ways. It is doubtless this difference that led [Roman] law to give girls a legal right that it denied to boys.

Maleville: The object of the law was to favor marriage.

Tronchet: Its goal was to temper the harshness of Roman paternal authority....

Jean-Etienne-Marie Portalis: Let us examine how the law was established. It was unknown as long as Rome preserved its republican morality, which the emperors tried to alter. To do this, they tried to weaken paternal authority, which was closely linked to the ancient morality of the Romans: the law had no other motives. Daughters rarely invoked it, but when they did, the father could not avoid exposing his affairs so that the amount of the obligatory dowry could be determined; thus, his resources and the advantages of the proposed marriage were discussed: everything was left to the judge's discretion.

In France, our legislation is divided: written law areas allowed dowry lawsuit; under customary law, it was rejected. What will happen if, in making the legislation uniform, we extend to areas of customary law the jurisprudence of written law? There will be a commotion that will not favor fathers, especially given the current decline of morality.... Barbarous fathers are not typical; it is more common that they love their children than that they are loved by them. This difference stems from what a kind of proprietary sentiment adds to the love that nature put in the heart of fathers....

Boulay: If fear of the barbarity of fathers determined our decision, it would overturn the whole system of paternal authority. The civil code strips fathers of the advantage they had, under written law, of exploiting their children's property until their emancipation; it is therefore fair to compensate them by freeing them from a legal action uniquely destined to temper their power, since the law is going to restrain its scope.

Consul Cambacérès: We cannot force all fathers to give their children dowries and establish them; but it would be strange that a formal prohibition prevents them from being obliged to do so. Reason and experience teach that there are fathers against whom this measure is necessary. We speak of immorality; it is found among fathers no less than children.... Thus, we must examine if, in the actual state of affairs, the courts should not have authority to force fathers to fulfill their obligations....

Michel-Louis-Etienne Regnaud de Saint-Jean-d'Angély (1762–1819): Rejecting the proposed draft would cause grave inconveniences. In written law areas, daughters can demand a dowry even after they are married and under the influence of husbands who naturally do not have the same respect and tenderness for the father as the daughter. Sometimes a self-interested man would marry a daughter without a dowry in the hope of then demanding one from the father, whom he would sue, in the name of his daughter....

Forging a New Elite

21

MILLOT DE FONTAINES

Letter of Recommendation for the Military School
July 14, 1810

Napoleon believed it essential to win over social elites. His efforts to restore order after 18 Brumaire went far toward achieving this end. But Napoleon sought more than passive acceptance of his rule. He wanted elites to serve his regime personally and identify their interests with his own. The ideas, assumptions, and spirit of the emerging Napoleonic elite can be discerned in the arguments and qualifications they themselves advanced when seeking government favors. The following letter of recommendation, for admission to the Saint-Cyr military school, is particularly revealing.

Archives Nationales, F^{17} 1740, Recommendation by Naval Ministry Department Head Millot de Fontaines.

Victor Bernard de Courville, former royal naval officer, from a family long devoted to state service, deceased in 1801 following an illness contracted aboard the vessels of the state, left, with a fortune greatly reduced by revolutionary events, four sons whose only ambition is to follow in their ancestors' footsteps.

Two are already serving. The eldest, an officer cadet in the Imperial Guard, is awaiting the reward he has merited through his education . . . and participation in the glorious campaigns of Austria, Prussia, Poland, and Spain. The second, aged 19, has just passed the examination to become a first-class naval aspirant after seven years' service.

The third and the youngest, Hypolite and Achille Bernard de Courville, one 17-and-a-half and the other 16 years of age, were admitted two years ago to the Lycée of Nantes by the protective government under which we have the good fortune to live. The debris of their inheritance had been consumed by their brothers' education and advancement. Their burning desire to embrace the career of arms was clouded by worry over how they might find the means to do so, when the instruction of His Excellency the Minister of War of the month of September 1809 rekindled hope and confidence in their hearts by promising scholarship students in the lycées free places in the military schools.

Today, now that their sense of having been sufficiently educated redoubles their ardor, now that the moment of conscription looms, I implore for them your benevolent protection. I beg you, My Lord, to recommend them to His Excellency the Minister of War for admission as scholarship students to Saint-Cyr.

This benefit, My Lord, will win you the undying gratitude of the two young men and their whole family.

22

MINISTRY OF WAR

Notes on Military School Applicants

August 1809

This list of applicants judged apt for admission to Saint-Cyr suggests the social pool from which the officer academy drew, its unspoken admissions criteria, and the degree to which Napoleon had succeeded in forming his dreamed-of elite.

Boussion: Father, was member of the Constituent Assembly; then president of several administrations; currently member of the prefectural council. Young Boussion is nephew of Monsieur de Grammont, former colonel of the Enghien regiment, who served 48 years and only left the service because of wounds.

Foy: Father is director of the Ham postal service. Paternal uncle is brigadier general and baron of the Empire.

De Villiers: Father, former mayor of Malines, was commissioner of the executive power in the criminal court, elector, and one of five departmental administrators.

Rapp: Father is tax collector. . . . The aspirant is nephew of General Rapp. His elder brother is a paying student at St-Cyr.

Pollet: Father died with the rank of captain; left his widow with five children. His uncle, a grenadier captain, was killed in Cyprus; merited a saber of honor. Another uncle is quarter-master decorated with the cross [of the Legion of Honor].

Rommel: Son of a master stone-cutter and public works entrepreneur of Brussels, is the second of 9 children.

Anthony: Son of a member of the general council of Dijon, former forge-master.

Colin: Father a merchant. Close relative of Landorny, under-prefect at Mondidier.

Crèvechamp: Father was lieutenant in the 6th Light-Horse regiment.

Archives Nationales, F[17] 6757.

Patissier: Father, an officer, retired after 15 years when he lost use of left arm. Little fortune.

Carbonnel: Father, artillery captain, served in campaigns of 1762, 1792, and 1793. Retired in the Year IX with a pension. Uncle is colonel-director of Imperial corps of artillery at Le Havre. Brother is officer in the 27th. Income of 941 francs per year.

Muyssard: Father, General Muyssard Desobeaux, served 64 years in the artillery. Brother is officer in the 75th. Very modest fortune.

Gaillard-Blairville: Great-grandfather had the cordon-rouge;[1] grandfather was artillery captain; his uncle, General Taviel, is commander-in-chief of the artillery in Spain. Brother is lieutenant in the 88th Infantry. The family can pay his tuition. His father, former alderman of St-Omer, is captain of its National Guard.

Martin: Son of a deceased former municipal officer and large landowner. Widowed mother has a considerable fortune.

Schwartz: Son of an officer retired after 10 years' service in the Hesse-Darmstadt regiment; two campaigns at sea. His uncle, General Schwartz, has 38 years' service, served in all the campaigns, and now commands the cavalry in Spain.

Jacob: Son of a public works entrepreneur and property-owner in Metz who was battalion commander of that city's National Guard. His fortune permits him to pay his son's tuition and an allowance.

Regnard: Son of a former metallurgical employee whose fortune and landed property are sufficient for the education of his children.

---

[1] *cordon-rouge*: An Old Regime decoration reserved for nobles.

Napoleonic Propaganda

23

NAPOLEON BONAPARTE

Letter to Minister of the Interior

May 30, 1807

For most of the population, the doors to Saint-Cyr and other prestigious "feeder" schools were effectively closed. Napoleon tried to attach such people to his regime by other means. He lavished vast sums on monumental architecture, heroic paintings, and other forms of propaganda designed to showcase his glory. The following document—a letter from Napoleon to his interior minister, Jean-Baptiste de Nompère de Champagny (1756–1834), on the design of a monument to the Grand Army—illustrates one of these initiatives.

Monsieur Vignon's [project] is the only one which fulfills my aim. I wanted a temple, not a church. How could we compete with St. Genevieve, Notre-Dame, and above all St. Peter's in Rome? Vignon's project has a number of advantages, including that of meshing better with the palace of the Legislative Body and not overwhelming the Tuileries. . . .

The spectators should be placed like I told you, on the marble benches forming the public amphitheaters; and the people required for the ceremonies will be placed on the benches in such a way as to underline their distinction.

Amphitheaters full of women will contrast with the grave and severe costume of the personages in the ceremony.

The orator's podium should be fixed and beautifully appointed. Nothing in this temple should be mobile and changing; on the contrary, everything should be fixed in its proper place. . . .

There must be no wood used in the construction of this temple. Why not use iron . . . for the vault? Wouldn't this material be preferable to

Correspondance de Napoléon: Six cents lettres de travail (1806–1810), ed. Maximilien Vox (Paris: Gallimard, 1943), 171–73.

wood? In a temple destined to last thousands of years, we must seek the greatest possible solidity, avoid any construction that could be questioned by the experts, and give the greatest attention to the choice of materials; granite and iron for this monument. One will object that the present columns are not of granite; but this objection is no good because, with time, we can replace them without hurting the monument. Yet, if granite would cost too much and produce excessive details, we should abandon it, because the principal condition of the project is that it be completed in three or four years, at most five.

This monument is political; it thus numbers among those that must be finished quickly. You should nonetheless look for granite for other monuments I will order and which, by their nature, can take thirty, forty, or fifty years to build.

I suppose that all the interior sculptures will be marble, and that no one will propose sculptures suited to salons and the dining rooms of Parisian bankers' wives. Anything that is not simple and noble is useless; anything that is not durable should be avoided in this monument.

24

NAPOLEON BONAPARTE

Executive Order

March 3, 1806

Below is the text of an order drafted by Napoleon that commissions several paintings. It specifies the theme and price of each work.

The following subjects will be painted, for the sums attributed to each:

1) The Emperor haranguing the 2nd corps on the Lech Bridge in Augsburg (12,000 francs).
2) The Austrian army leaving Ulm as prisoners of war, filing

Correspondance de Napoléon: Six cents lettres de travail (1806–1810), ed. Maximilien Vox (Paris: Gallimard, 1943), 182–3.

before His Majesty while he addresses the defeated generals (12,000).

3) The surprise attack on the Danube Bridge at Vienna... (12,000).

4) Charge of the Russian Imperial Guards; Rapp presenting the Emperor with flags, cannons, Prince Repnine, and more than 800 noble prisoners of the Russian guard (12,000).

5) Interview of the Emperor Napoleon and the Emperor Francis II in Moravia (12,000).

6) The 76th demi-brigade recovering its flags from the Army of Innsbruck (12,000).

7) The Emperor pardoning the rebels of Cairo on Ezbeckych Place (12,000).

8) The assemblies of Lyon ... (12,000).

9) His Majesty's entry into Munich and welcome by the Bavarians (6,000).

10) The marriage of His Royal Highness the Prince Eugene with Princess Augusta of Bavaria (6,000).

11) Crossing of the Suez Isthmus, and His Majesty visiting the Fountains of Moses (6,000).

12) The arrival and interview of His Majesty with His Holiness at Fontainebleau ... (6,000).

13) The Virgin of Victory ... (6,000).

14) The fight of the *Formidable*, commanded by Gilles Troude at Algeciras, who dismasted an English vessel and forced Admiral Saumarez to abandon it, even though he had four vessels (8,000).

25

Evolving Images of Napoleon's Power
1797–1812

Throughout his career, Napoleon was acutely aware of the power of images over the political imagination. He thus paid a great deal of attention to crafting images of himself as a ruler capable of inspiring obedience, loyalty, and even devotion. Together with this book's cover illustration, the following selection of paintings, commissioned between 1797 and 1812, reveals the evolution of Napoleon's visual self-representation.

BONAPARTE

KAROLVS MAGNVS IMP

(Opposite) Jacques-Louis David, Le Premier Consul franchissant les Alpes au col du Grand-Saint-Bernard, *1801*

Jacques-Louis David (1748–1825) was the most influential painter of revolutionary and Napoleonic France. By the 1770s, he had already won international recognition for his works in the neoclassical style—a style that harmonized with the revolutionary ethos. He became a strong supporter of the Revolution and sought to advance its fortunes through paintings that stressed republican virtue. After Brumaire, David became an ardent supporter of the Napoleonic regime, depicting the glory of its ruler in numerous propagandistic works of high quality. David's depiction of Napoleon crossing the Alps contributed powerfully to forging the Napoleonic myth.

Antoine-Jean Gros (1771–1835) was one of David's most talented pupils. He entered David's studio in 1785 and continued to work with his mentor during the early years of the Revolution. But in 1793 accusations of royalism forced Gros to flee from France to Italy. It was there in 1796 that he met Napoleon and held the brief portrait session that served as the basis for his most famous work, *Le General Bonaparte à Arcole* (see the cover illustration). After Napoleon came to power, Gros continued to paint works glorifying the new regime and its master. In this painting, Gros reveals a different image of Napoleon than that expressed in works celebrating his military accomplishments.

(Opposite) Jacques-Louis David, Le serment de l'armée après la distribution des aigles, *1805*

This lesser-known work of David portrays Napoleon's distribution of standards to his army in a ceremony held several days after the imperial coronation. It draws upon neoclassical imagery to celebrate the military ethos of the imperial regime. It seeks to establish a parallel between the military tradition of imperial Rome, in which each legion received a standard topped by the figure of an eagle, and the regiments of France. In return for these new emblems, the soldiers are swearing an oath of loyalty to their new emperor. How does this painting represent the relationship between the new emperor and the French army? Does this represent the continuation of France's revolutionary military tradition or a new departure?

Réunion des Musées Nationaux/Art Resource, N.Y.

(Opposite) François-Pascal-Simon Gérard, Napoléon en grand habillement du Sacre, *1805*

François-Pascal-Simon Gérard (1770–1837) was one of David's many students. Born in Rome to a French father and an Italian mother, Gérard entered David's studio in 1786. This portrait of Napoleon in his coronation robes is intended to project an image of imperial majesty that contrasts with some of the more dynamic depictions of Napoleon. Do you think it is successful in doing so? What kind of impression are the emperor's expression and physical bearing, his clothing, and the objects with which he is portrayed intended to convey?

Réunion des Musées Nationaux/Art Resource, N.Y.

(Opposite) *Engraved Reproduction of Maurice Orange,* Après la victoire, *undated*

Created by Maurice Orange (1868–1916), this mass-produced print offers an image of Napoleon that contrasts sharply with those paintings emphasizing his military glory (page 88) or imperial dignity (pages 86 and 90). In it, Napoleon is dressed in a simple military overcoat and is sharing a pinch of snuff with a loyal old soldier of his imperial guard. To whom might this image have appealed? What political message might it be intended to send? Which sort of images—those emphasizing Napoleon's imperial dignity or those portraying him in a more modest light—resonate most with you?

(Opposite) Jean-Nicholas Laugier, Engraved Reproduction of Jacques-Louis David's Napoléon dans son étude, *1812*

This mass-produced reproduction of David's portrait of Napoleon in his study reveals yet another facet of Napoleon's evolving, multidimensional image. What is it intended to say about the emperor? Note particularly his expression, the clothing he is wearing, the setting, and the many telling background details (the clock, the candles, the papers). What has Napoleon just finished doing? What is this image trying to say about Napoleon as head of state? How does this message compare with that expressed by the other paintings depicting Napoleon as ruler of France (pages 84–90)?

26

The Imperial Catechism

1808

This document is an extract from the Imperial Catechism, *published in 1808 and approved by the papal legate to France. It offers one example of how Napoleon tried to make Catholicism work for his regime.*

Q: What are the duties of Christians to the princes who govern them, and what are our specific duties to Napoleon I, our Emperor?

A: Christians owe their princes, and we particularly owe Napoleon I, our Emperor, love, respect, obedience, loyalty, military service, the tributes demanded for the preservation and defense of the Empire and his throne; we also owe him fervent prayers for his safety and for the State's spiritual and temporal prosperity.

Q: Why must we fulfill all these duties to our Emperor?

A: First, because God, who creates empires and distributes them at will, by lavishing gifts on our Emperor, in peace and war, made him our sovereign and made him the minister of His power and image on earth. Thus, to honor and serve our Emperor is to honor and serve God himself. . . .

Q: Are there particular reasons that should attach us even more closely to Napoleon I, our Emperor?

A: Yes, because it is he whom God chose in difficult circumstances to reestablish and protect the public worship of the holy religion of our fathers. He restored and maintained public order by his profound and active wisdom; he defends the State with his powerful arm; he became the Lord's anointed by the consecration he received from the Sovereign Pontiff, head of the Universal Church.

Q: What should we think of those who neglect their duties toward our Emperor?

A: According to the Apostle Paul, they are resisting the divinely ordained order and condemning themselves to eternal damnation.

Q: Do our duties toward our Emperor also bind us to his legitimate successors, in the order established by the Imperial constitutions?

Marcelle and Lucien Dechappe, *L'Histoire par les textes*, vol. 2, *Révolution et Empire* (Paris: Delaharpe, 1928), 338–39.

A: Yes, without a doubt; because we read in the Holy Scripture that God, Lord of Heaven and Earth, by his supreme will and Providence gives empires not only to one person in particular, but to his entire family.

The Secret Police

27

Paris Police Reports
1804–1807

Napoleon did not assume that propaganda alone could win over the French population. He also maintained an imposing secret police organization, whose agents closely monitored the content of the press and theater, the doings of counterrevolutionary and radical activists, labor unrest, morality, and even priests' sermons. This selection of police reports indicates the scope of its activities.

OCTOBER 18, 1804

The direction given to the newspapers has produced on most of them an effect very advantageous to the views of His Majesty and the good of his government. There are only three left which retain any partisan coloration: the *French Citizen*, the *Journal of Debates*, and the *Mercure*. The first has no spirit and almost no subscribers.... The *Mercure* sometimes contains articles written with talent, but they are generally dictated by passion and in a sense contrary to the government's intentions. The *Journal of Debates*, still faithful to its plan, preaches with audacious stubbornness intolerance and proscription of all the men of the Revolution. ... It must be noted that this journal is not the work of an individual, but of many writers, all animated by the same spirit and

Alphonse Aulard, *Paris sous le Premier Empire* (Paris: various publishers, 1912–1923). Documents are in the following order: vol. 1,327–28; vol. 2, 12; vol. 2, 425–26; vol. 2, 714–26; vol. 3, 226–27; vol. 3, 432.

directed by the same principles. The *French Citizen* seeks to excite fanaticism of philosophy; the two others want to revive that of religion. The first could create new Brutuses; the others could sharpen the daggers of Jacques Clément or renew the scenes of the Jesuits in Portugal.

JUNE 20, 1805

The police discovered a highly secret gathering, similar to the Roman Saturnalia, which took place every Thursday from dusk to midnight in a house in Vaugirard Street, no. 102. To gain admission, one had to be initiated, give the password, and pay 12 francs. . . . One was then introduced into a vast, entirely darkened room, where one found a number of half-naked ladies and, in total silence, one could indulge in unrestrained debauchery with the first one encountered. Married women of all ranks and backgrounds, swept up by raging passion or libertinism, secretly went to that house, where they could give themselves over to their passion without fear. The men were expressly instructed not to try to discover either the features or the social status of the women they met there and, even more firmly, not to follow them after leaving. . . . Last night we succeeded in infiltrating an agent into the gathering and, at a given moment, police officers burst in with lights. They found a number of men and women in the greatest disorder. Among the men were particularly noted Barizon, ex-banker, Hugot, department head in the Council of State, the ex-marquis de Castellane, Grenier, lawyer in the Appeals Court, etc. Regarding the women, most were young shop girls, workers, and the 19-year-old niece of a lawyer.

FEBRUARY 5, 1806

The New Awakening of Epiménide, a little allegorical play about the peace, was performed yesterday, with great success, at the Louvois Theater. Epiménide, who fell asleep in the Year VII [1798], believes he is still living at this time, when all the most essential institutions were at the mercy of different systems. He is told that things have changed prodigiously since his sleep, and he thinks he has slept not just a few years, as he is told, but for several centuries, so miraculous seem to him the changes France has undergone since being governed by Napoleon. The state of astonishment into which Epiménide falls produces a number of allusions, all of which were covered with applause; a word referring to the rapidity of the most recent conquests was received with almost indescribable enthusiasm: "Monsieur (a young lady, whose lover was at the Battle of Austerlitz and is expected to return at any moment, asks her geography teacher), does it take a long time to return here from Vienna?" "Mademoiselle," responds the geography teacher, "it takes a lot longer to return than to go there." Couplets to the glory of His Majesty the Emperor and in praise of Her Majesty the Empress close the play and blended into serenade in which villagers decorate with laurels the arms of the warriors; all of this drew enthusiastic applause, and most of the couplets were demanded and repeated. The play's authors were named to the acclamations of the public: they are Etienne and Nanteuil, known for other successes.

OCTOBER 5, 6, 9, AND 12, 1806

For three days, the construction workers have grumbled about the police ordinance that determines the length of workdays and meal-times. . . . According to some of the mutineers, "they treat us like beasts of burden, etc." We think these insinuations were reinforced by subaltern entrepreneurs jealous of the directors of the large public workshops. Today, the men working on the Imperial Palace, Legislature, and other public edifices refused to work; 27 of the most mutinous were arrested in the middle of groups they were haranguing and trying to excite; they were imprisoned at the Bicetre. Others dispersed and did not go to work. We are watching those who stayed at home and in cabarets near their workshops. All workers in private enterprises worked as usual, as the masters have not yet changed the hours of work and meals. . . .

The building workers on government projects persist in refusing to work and accept the regulation that fixes the hours of their labor and meals. The police prefect had three of these workers arrested yesterday; this brings to 30 the number of arrests. This morning, nine of those detained agreed to return to work and were released. It does not appear that this convinced any others to return, and the workshops remain as empty as yesterday. A poster insulting the interior ministry and police prefecture was seen this morning on the walls of the Tuileries Palace. . . . The workers' main grievance . . . is the article giving them only a one-hour break, 10 to 11 AM in winter, which makes them work continuously for six to seven hours without eating. It is the same as the old pre-revolutionary regulations, over which [the more generous revolutionary work regulation] has prevailed for 15 years. All masters want to see it executed; but only those who work for the government are determined to enforce it. . . .

The public works are still deserted. About 600–700 workers assembled this morning on the Place de Grève to sell their services to other entrepreneurs. . . . Order was maintained; but there was more bitterness than before. . . .

The builders came to work today in greater numbers than during the preceding days. Some of those who had been arrested were freed and are now working. Others came as the day went on. They had lunch from 10 to 11 AM. . . .

JUNE 25, 1807

I arrested three discharged ex-soldiers . . . for having spoken of an insurrection which is supposed to take place in Paris, for having bragged of their party's strength, and for having boasted of their illustrious leaders. These three individuals are called Calendini, Martin, and Lambert. Calendini was born . . . in the department of Golo. Before the Revolution he served in the Royal-Corsica regiment. During the Revolution, he rose to the rank of adjutant-general and was discharged seven years ago. When he was arrested, we found his room decorated with slogans like "Liberty or Death," portraits of Robespierre and Mucius Scaevola. The second, named Martin, was born in the Vaucluse. He was a battalion commander discharged in the Year X. The third, Lambert, was born at Tours. He was discharged in the Year VIII with the rank of adjutant-general. . . . As such men can only be dangerous at Paris, I think they should be sent at least 120 miles away.

NOVEMBER 26, 1807

The *Priests' Journal* has published an excerpt from a sermon pronounced at Versailles by the Abbé de Boulogne, in which there are several inconvenient passages, including this one: "France will be happy . . . if, repentant of her crazy errors . . . she fully realizes that true glory lies not in conquering but in establishing, not in destroying but in preserving . . . that it is a thousand times grander to protect a hospice or home for the poor, than to build a temple to the Lord or school for his ministers, than to take and bestow scepters and crowns; and that even one of these holy works . . . is a thousand times more valuable in the eyes of the truly wise than all these brilliant trophies and monuments to glory that blind our eyes." The minister expressed his discontent to the editor for having allowed the publication of such a piece, especially now when the return of the Imperial Guard inspires such enthusiasm for your victories. The editor excused himself on the grounds that he did not feel authorized to correct a sermon preached by one of His Majesty's almoners before the bishop and prefect of Versailles.

4

From Republic to Empire

Legion of Honor

28

PIERRE-LOUIS ROEDERER

Speech Proposing the Creation of a Legion of Honor
May 9, 1802

With the onset of peace in 1802, the regime appeared more secure than ever. But Napoleon worried, for its stability rested on little more than his own energy and genius. If he were to die, he feared, it would collapse in a welter of bloody strife. He concluded that the regime's survival required a new elite committed to him personally. A major step toward this goal was the creation of the Legion of Honor, a corps whose members would be chosen by Napoleon himself from among his most devoted followers and state servants. The following document is an excerpt from the speech of Pierre-Louis Roederer proposing the creation of the Legion of Honor.

The proposed Legion of Honor is an institution to reinforce our republican laws and solidify the Revolution.

It pays military and civil service with the prize of courage they have all merited; it unites them in the same glory. . . .

It joins by a common distinction men already united by honorable memories; it nourishes sweet affection among men already disposed to love one another by a reciprocal esteem.

It places the laws which preserve equality, liberty, and property under their consideration and protection.

It erases the distinctions of nobility that placed inherited glory ahead of acquired glory, and the descendants of great men before great men themselves.

It is a moral institution which adds force and activity to the sentiment of honor, which so powerfully moves the French nation.

It is a political institution which establishes in society intermediaries through whom acts of government will be faithfully communicated to public opinion . . . and public opinion will rise to the government.

It is a military institution that will attract to our armies that [wealthy] portion of French youth who would otherwise be drawn to a life of idle ease. . . .

Finally, it is the creation of a new currency of a very different value than the Treasury's money; a currency whose title is unalterable and whose mine cannot be exhausted because it resides in French honor; finally, a currency which can alone reward actions considered superior to all rewards.

29

JACQUES-FORTUNAT SAVOYE-ROLLIN

Speech Opposing the Creation of a Legion of Honor
May 12, 1802

The proposal to create a Legion of Honor troubled many politicians, who felt that it threatened republican equality. A significant number spoke against the measure. The following excerpt from a speech by Jacques-Fortunat Savoye-Rollin (1754–1823) gives a sense of the arguments mobilized against the creation of the Legion of Honor.

Archives Parlementaires, series II, vol. 3, 718–20.

Since its foundation, the Tribunate has never considered a more important law, . . . a law which attacks the foundation of public liberty.

What is the law's stated goal? To distribute rewards to soldiers and civil servants who have rendered great services to the Republic. What means does it employ? The organization of a Legion of Honor composed of 6,000 lifetime legionnaires, which will gradually fill vacancies by initiating those who have merited military and civil distinctions.

This means is visibly alien to the law's goal. It is completely obvious that it is unnecessary to create a privileged body to reward the defenders of a Republic. . . .

The institution of a Legion of Honor directly contradicts the letter and spirit of the constitution: the letter, because it does not authorize the creation of a military body distinguished from the regular land and sea forces by extraordinary functions and prerogatives; the spirit, because in a representative constitution, the division of powers cannot be altered. If the proposed intermediate body participated in all the powers, as we are led to believe, its very confusion would make it unconstitutional; if it had prerogatives without power, it would still be unconstitutional because it would violate equality of rights; a free state has but one order of citizens and magistrates; if this corps had neither power nor prerogatives, it would be useless. . . .

I will argue that, by creating among yourselves this legion, you are accepting a patrician class which will continually tend to become a hereditary and military nobility. . . .

Of all the causes that produced the French Revolution, the most remarkable . . . was the division which reigned among the different orders of the State.

The order which was the last in rank had become, in the course of two centuries of active commerce and flourishing industry, the first by its wealth and knowledge; yet, the nobility still struggled advantageously against it, by asserting its privileges and monopoly of almost all grand positions. . . .

It was only after twelve years of frightful evils, but in the holiest and most just cause, that the Republic triumphed, that, guided by one of those rare men without whom revolutions never finish, it can finally harvest in the bosom of peace the fruits acquired so dearly: will it imprudently risk losing them by admitting among its constituted powers a body harboring all the germs of the inequality of conditions?

Effectively, the Legion of Honor lacks none of the elements which founded, among all peoples, hereditary nobility: we find in it particular attributions of political power, honors, titles, and fixed revenues. . . .

Obviously, this Legion will reproduce poorly-extinguished preju-
dices. . . . Its most real vice . . . is to absolutely reestablish barbarian
ideas, in which all powers derived from military authority. It is a fundamental principle of feudalism that those who were militarily subordinated to someone were also under his civil jurisdiction; . . . in this
order of things, the civil power, completely subordinated, knew only
military denominations, only military rewards; some feeble traces
remained under the Old Regime. . . . But today it would directly injure
the principles of a free government to imagine conferring, under the
guise of rewards, military ranks to magistrates like they still do in the
Ottoman Porte and Russia. . . .

We must thus see in the proposed law only what it precisely contains: a pure military corporation without functions. . . .

But, as a military institution, it is destructive of public liberty
because it creates a privileged order whose secret tendency is hereditary nobility, . . . because personal distinctions, just like hereditary
ones, introduce a particularistic spirit into the general spirit, separate
citizens from citizens, and sow between them the germs of confusion
and discord.

The New Dynasty

30

JEAN-FRANÇOIS CURÉE

Motion to Institute Hereditary Government
April 30, 1804

---

*Even after becoming Consul-for-Life in August 1802, Napoleon was not
satisfied. He dreamed of donning a crown and founding a dynasty. In
early 1804, after the discovery of new assassination plots intensified concerns about governmental stability, Napoleon judged the moment ripe to*

---

cast aside the republican trappings of his rule and assume the throne. When an obscure deputy, Jean-François Curée (1756–1835), proposed establishing hereditary government, the Tribunate approved the measure almost unanimously. Below is an excerpt from Curée's motion.

The success and longevity of any political system depends on government stability. . . . This principle is valid for all times and circumstances. But its application is even more urgent when, great changes in the States having created [a new order of things], one can demonstrate convincingly that the reestablishment of a sure, authentic, and hereditary course of succession in the Government associated with these outcomes and linked to them like a tree to its roots would sanction these political changes for the centuries and forever ensure the maintenance of these grand results. . . .

The noble movements which animated the French people in 1789 were principally directed against feudal institutions; yet, we committed the grave error of allowing supreme power to remain in the hands of an essentially feudal family. . . . King of France, Louis XVI never wanted to be King of the French: born sovereign, he could not truly accept becoming a magistrate. Your Charter was violated as soon as it was proclaimed; and in the midst of a general war, anarchy followed the horrifying collapse of the throne.

While the Constituent Assembly made the mistake of not bringing a new dynasty to the new order of things, far be it from me to blame it for this error. The Revolution was just beginning; no great reputation capable of inspiring their confidence had yet arisen. . . .

General Bonaparte touched French shores. Since then, we have constantly enjoyed the fruits of a wise, foresightful, and tireless administration. At what time, in what nation have the treasury's accounts and finances been established with . . . more scrupulous exactitude? Has not glorious peace been conquered? . . . Has not the Civil Code, the most complete and methodical system of legislation ever, emerged majestically from the learned and laborious discussions of legal scholars and statesmen, and spread knowledge of civil rights to the people? In a word, everything the people wanted in 1789 has been reestablished. Equality has been maintained. Law, which alone can impose charges on citizens for the good of the State, has been respected. The administration has severely rebuffed all threats to the irrevocability of the sale of national properties and the rights of their purchasers.

Finally, the altar has been raised up, and religion sanctified at the same time as liberty of conscience.

In this happy situation, where the French people possess all the rights they sought in the Revolution of 1789, only uncertainty for the future still troubles the State. . . .

What guarantee can we offer? . . . Heredity of power in a family whom the Revolution has made illustrious, whom equality and liberty have consecrated; heredity in the family of a leader who was the Republic's first soldier before becoming its first magistrate; of a leader whose civil qualities alone would have eminently distinguished him had he not filled the entire world with the sound of his arms and brilliance of his victories. . . .

Thus, an eternal barrier will protect us from the return of both the factions that tore us apart and the house we proscribed in 1792 because it had violated our rights; the house we proscribe today because it initiated against us foreign and civil war; which made torrents of French blood flow in the Vendée; . . . which has been for so many years the general source of the troubles and disasters that have torn apart our country. . . .

In voting for the heredity of a leader . . . we will prevent the return of a master.

31

LAZARE CARNOT

Speech against Curée's Motion

May 1, 1804

The following document is excerpted from a speech by Lazare Carnot (1753–1823), a former member of the Committee of Public Safety and the Executive Directory. A committed republican, he was the only tribune to combat Curée's motion.

Archives Parlementaires, series II, vol. 8, 288–90.

. . . I do not seek to attenuate the praise given to the First Consul; if we owed him only the Civil Code, his name would deserve to pass into posterity. But whatever services a citizen has been able to provide his fatherland, there are limits that national honor and reason impose on public thankfulness. If this citizen has restored public liberty, if he has saved his country, would the sacrifice of that same liberty truly be a reward?

From the moment the French people were asked to vote on the life consulate, everyone could easily see unspoken considerations, ulterior motives.

In effect, we have seen a succession of obviously monarchical institutions; each [has been justified with assurances] . . . that these institutions were only intended to give [liberty] the greatest possible protection.

Today the ultimate goal of all these preliminary steps has been revealed: we are asked to pronounce upon the formal proposition to reestablish the monarchical system and confer imperial and hereditary dignity on the First Consul. . . .

I will vote against the reestablishment of monarchy. . . .

All the arguments yet advanced for the reestablishment of monarchy in France boil down to the assertion that, without it, there is no means of ensuring governmental stability and public tranquility, of escaping from internal discord, of uniting against foreign enemies; that we vainly tried the republican system in every way possible; that the only result of these different efforts was anarchy, prolonged revolution, . . . constant fear of new disorders, and consequently a universal and profound desire to see hereditary government reestablished. . . .

We have been unable to establish among ourselves a republican regime, even though we have tried to under more or less democratic forms. But it must be noted that, of all the constitutions successively and unsuccessfully tried, all were created in the heat of factionalism and were the work of circumstances as imperious as they were fleeting: this is why they all failed. But since 18 Brumaire, we have entered a period, perhaps unique in the annals of the world, in which, sheltered from the storm, we can reflect calmly on how to establish liberty on a solid basis. After the Peace of Amiens, Bonaparte could have chosen between the republican and monarchical system; he could have done as he liked, he would not have met the slightest opposition. He was entrusted with our liberty; if he had fulfilled the nation's hopes, which thought him alone capable of resolving the great problem of public liberty in vast states, he would have won incomparable glory. . . .

It is quite true that before 18 Brumaire, the state was falling apart and that absolute power pulled it back from the edge of the abyss; but what should we conclude from it? What everyone knows: that political bodies are subject to illnesses that can only be cured by violent means, that temporary dictatorship is sometimes necessary to save liberty. . . .

[In the absence of factions, in calm times] . . . it is easier to form a republic without anarchy than a monarchy without despotism; all limitations would be illusory in a government whose head holds all executive force in his hands and disposes of all positions [in the state]. . . . Until now, we have invented nothing to temper supreme power except what are called intermediate or privileged bodies. But isn't this remedy worse than the problem? After all, absolute power only takes away liberty, whereas the institution of privileged bodies strips both liberty and equality. . . .

Doubtless, there would be no hesitation over the choice of a hereditary leader if it were necessary to give ourselves one: it would be absurd to draw a parallel between the First Consul and the pretenders of a family fallen under well-earned disdain and whose vindictive and bloodthirsty dispositions are only too well known. To restore the Bourbon house would renew the frightful scenes of the revolution, and proscription would inevitably extend itself over the property and persons of nearly all citizens. But excluding this dynasty does not imply the need for a new one. . . .

. . . My heart tells me that liberty is possible, that its regime is easy and more stable than any arbitrary government, than any oligarchy.

The Imperial Court

32

EMMANUEL-AUGUSTE DE LAS CASES

Reestablishment of Court Etiquette

undated

With the restoration of monarchical government came the reestablishment of a court. But the Imperial Court differed in significant ways from that of the Bourbons. In this selection, one of Napoleon's former chamberlains, Emmanuel-Auguste, comte de Las Cases (1766–1842), describes how, in meeting the challenge of rebuilding a court in postrevolutionary France, Napoleon created a new kind of court culture.

Acceding to sovereign power, Napoleon found a [blank slate] . . . and could form a Court at will. He sought . . . a reasonable compromise by seeking to harmonize the dignity of the throne with our new mores and, above all, by making this creation work to ameliorate the manners of the grandees and industriousness of the people. It was certainly no small matter to erect a throne on the same terrain where the reigning monarch had been legally executed and where a constitutional oath of hatred for kings was annually sworn. It was no small matter to reestablish dignities, titles, and decorations amidst a people who had for fifteen years been fighting and triumphing to proscribe them. All the same, Napoleon, who always seemed to do what he wanted, because he was a master of the art of the possible, overcame these difficulties. He was made Emperor, he created for himself dignitaries and a Court. Soon, victory seemed to take charge of reinforcing and illustrating this new order of things. All Europe recognized it, and for a moment one would have said that all the Courts of the continent were flocking to Paris to compose that of the Tuileries, which became

Emmanuel-Auguste, comte de Las Cases, *Mémoires de Napoléon Ier* (Mémorial de Sainte-Hélène), vol. 5 (Paris: Cocuaud, n.d.), 47–55.

the most brilliant and numerous ever seen. It had social circles, ballets, performances; an extraordinary magnificence and splendor was deployed. Only the person of the sovereign retained an extreme simplicity, which served to help distinguish him. This luxury, the pomp he encouraged around him, reflected his plans, but not his tastes. [They] were calculated to stimulate our national productions and industry. The ceremonies and festivals for the marriage of the Empress and baptism of the King of Rome far surpassed everything that came before and, probably, will come.

The Emperor's goal was to restore on the outside everything that could harmonize with the other courts of Europe; but domestically, he was careful to adjust the old forms to accord with our new mores.

Thus, he reestablished royal *levées* and *couchers*;[1] but, instead of being real, they were purely nominal. Instead of presenting the smallest details of a true *toilette* and the unhygienic episodes it could entail, under the Emperor these moments were devoted to receiving or taking leave of those members of his household who had to take direct orders from him and whose prerogative was to be able to speak personally with him at these privileged times.

Thus, the Emperor reestablished special presentations to his person, admissions to his Court; but instead of deciding on official *proofs* of nobility, it was only on the combined basis of fortune, influence, and services.

Thus, the Emperor created titles which sounded like feudal ones; but . . . without prerogatives or privileges, they were open to all kinds of birth, services, and professions. . . .

Thus, the Emperor restored decorations and distributed crosses and cordons; but instead of granting them only to special and privileged classes, he extended them to the whole society, to all kinds of service, to all sorts of talent. . . .

It was the faithful and voluntary practice of the maxims [incarnated in these ceremonials] that made him a truly national monarch and would have made [his dynasty] . . . truly constitutional. . . .

---

[1] Ceremonies held in the monarch's bedchamber upon his rising in the morning and retiring in the evening.

33

Guide to Imperial Etiquette

1811

Although the new regime tried to rally former courtiers of the Bourbon dynasty and place them in their former positions, many members of the Imperial Court were of modest background. Stalwarts and comrades-in-arms from revolutionary days, they lacked the polish and sophistication to cut a fine figure in the new court. The following extract from a popular manual of courtly etiquette hints offered them guidance.

Everybody knows that one must write to grandees and other superiors differently than to equals; but there are many people who do not pay enough attention to the relations that may exist between them and those to whom they write, and there are even many who entirely overlook the personal qualities of others.

The details which follow should not appear daunting: the mind can instantly grasp in an instant what requires many words to express.

1) The relations between the writer and the intended recipient of the letter. Do you know each other? Have you written before? Are you friends? Or do you imagine, to the contrary, that you are enemies? And even if there is no reason to think so, do you think the recipient is indifferent to you? One ought to consider as well relations of age, family, and, in assessing the superiority of someone else, should pay attention not only to birth and rank, but also to wealth, merit, and influence.

I say influence, because there are people to whom one owes particular respect because they have the ear of grandees. One often sees them treated with great respect not only by their equals, but also by those to whom they are very inferior: it would be a great mistake to treat such people with unaccustomed familiarity.

I also say wealth: this quality does not give rank; but how many people suppose that it does! In this instance, opinion takes the place of

---

Le secrétaire de la Cour Impériale de France, ou modèles de placets, pétitions, et lettres adressées à l'Empereur (Paris: Barba, 1811), 243–46.

truth: in any event, vanity is the nearly inseparable companion of wealth; and rich people always believe themselves superior to people of their own rank who have less.

With regard to merit, it is not always known; but when it has been discovered, we ought to honor it.

2) The qualities of the person to whom one writes. Is he of high birth, of distinguished rank? Is he famous or unknown? Is he very busy or does he have much leisure time? Is he serious and austere or of a joyous humor? Of a gentle disposition or easily angered? Proud or modest? Easygoing or rigid and punctilious? These different qualities require more or less circumspection: one should be concise with very busy people and reserved with serious ones; one should treat grandees respectfully, although without cringing; and as they are always occupied with many amusements, one should proceed in the same way with them as with people who have many occupations; respect the refinement of the ones, profit with moderation from the relaxed disposition of the others; always adjust yourself to the character of each.

34

CHARLES-MAURICE DE TALLEYRAND

Napoleon's Austrian Marriage

1853

Once he became emperor, Napoleon grew worried about his lack of a son to inherit the throne. The birth of a son to his Polish mistress, Maria Waleska, convinced him that Josephine was no longer capable of bearing children. Napoleon divorced her on December 15, 1809, and sought a new, younger spouse whose grandeur would complement his own. The following extract, from the memoirs of Charles-Maurice de Talleyrand-Périgord (1754–1838), the noted diplomat who served as Napoleon's foreign minister, describes the extraordinary council meeting in January 1810 in which Napoleon settled his choice on the Habsburg princess Marie-Louise of Austria (1791–1847).

Charles-Maurice de Talleyrand, *Mémoires du Prince de Talleyrand*, vol. 2 (Paris: Henri Javal, 1953), 39–41.

Napoleon: "It is with regret that I have renounced a union [with Josephine] which so sweetened my home life. If . . . I consulted only my own feelings, I would choose my new spouse among the young charges of the Legion of Honor,[1] daughters of the brave men of France. I would thereby give the French an Empress whose qualities and virtues would make her most worthy of the throne. But we must bend to the customs of our century, to the practice of other States, and above all to the course political duty dictates. Sovereigns have sought marriage with my relatives. I believe there is none now to whom I could not confidently offer my personal alliance. Three reigning families could give France an empress; the Russian, Austrian, and Saxon. I have assembled you to examine which of these three alliances is in the best interest of the Empire."

The long silence which followed this discourse was broken by the Emperor who asked: "Monsieur Arch-Chancellor, what is your opinion?"

Cambacérès, who seemed to have prepared what he was going to say, found in his recollections as a former member of the Committee of Public Safety, that Austria was and always would be our enemy. After having developed at length this idea, which he supported with many facts and precedents, he concluded that the Emperor should marry a Grand Duchess of Russia.

Lebrun mobilized all the arguments of habit, education, and simplicity to recommend the Court of Saxony, and voted for that alliance. Murat and Fouché thought the interests of the Revolution would be safer with a Russian alliance. It seems both felt more comfortable with the descendants of the Czars than those of Rudolph of Habsburg.

My turn came; I was on familiar terrain; I performed sufficiently well. I advanced excellent reasons why an Austrian alliance would be preferable for France. My secret concern was that the survival of Austria depended on the Emperor's decision. But this was not the place to say it. Having briefly exposed the pros and cons of a Russian and an Austrian marriage, I came out in favor of the latter. I addressed myself to the Emperor as a Frenchman, requesting that an Austrian princess appear among us to absolve France in the eyes of Europe and her own eyes of a crime which was not of her doing, but was entirely the deed of a faction. The term "European reconciliation" that I employed several times, pleased several members of the council, who were tired of war. Despite some objections the Emperor made to me, I saw that my advice suited him.

---

[1] A reference to the girls at Ecouen, a state-run boarding school reserved for the daughters of legionnaires.

The Imperial Nobility

35

NAPOLEON BONAPARTE

Speech to the Senate
on the Creation of Imperial Duchies
1807

With the foundation of the empire, the Legion of Honor no longer pro-vided a sufficient social basis for the regime. Most of its members, chosen for their services, were of modest wealth and social background. More-over, as their distinction was only personal, they had no direct interest in ensuring the transmission of the imperial dignity to Napoleon's son. Hereditary government, Napoleon believed, required a hereditary social elite—a nobility—that would protect the imperial succession in order to maintain its own hereditary status. And this was just one of many bene-fits the creation of an imperial nobility was intended to bring. The follow-ing document is a speech addressed to the Senate in 1807 proposing the creation of duchies to reward Napoleon's marshals.

For the stability of our throne and brilliance of our crown, for the greatest benefit of our peoples, it is necessary to grant titles to the most distinguished citizens to whom we owe a debt of gratitude for the homeland's prosperity. . . . A nation is not completely organized . . . if the means of reward are not proportionate to the services its citi-zens are called upon to render. Monetary rewards would be onerous to our peoples and would not correspond to the sentiments which stimulate good service and inspire grand actions. If wealth is honor-able when it is the fruit of labor and a long and useful career, it is shameful when it comes from fraud, monopoly, or corruption. It is thus necessary to distinguish and raise up by titles, honorably

Archives Nationales, AF IV 1040.

acquired fortunes. It is also in harmony with all the sentiments of the human heart to permit the transmission of titles which, by recommending the sons of those who served well, will impose upon them the duty of sacrificing everything for the honor of the fatherland and glory of our throne. We have also considered that if these rewards were granted only to military service, we would harm the civil services that prepare more quietly but with equal merit, the prosperity of the State and triumph of our armies. . . .

Titles that would give hereditary rights to employment or which would grant rights of jurisdiction and vassalage over our subjects would injure the dignity of the French. Equal before the law, they are all under our jurisdiction. Whether they contribute to the prosperity of this vast Empire by professing the arts and sciences, practicing agriculture and commerce, serving the state in the tribunals, administrations or armies, whether rich or poor, magistrates or simple citizens, they have an equal right to our affection. Our most treasured thought is to view them all as our children.

The members of the Senate will still be chosen among the most distinguished citizens. We will let no other consideration govern our choice than personal service. The order of advancement and military hierarchy will not be changed, and any soldier will be able to rise from the lowest to the highest rank if he has merited it by the brilliance or length of his services.

Finally, we have considered that imperial titles alone can efface the memory of the feudal titles that the will of our peoples has forever destroyed.

36

NAPOLEON BONAPARTE

Letter to Cambacérès

June 14, 1810

Napoleon expected the creation of an imperial nobility to reconcile the principal members of the Old Regime aristocracy to his regime. In the following letter from Napoleon to his Arch-Chancellor Cambacérès, Napoleon discusses the fusion of old and new nobilities.

We must make all of France benefit from the institution of hereditary titles. If we do not, this institution will never be national; it will not make [the nation] forget those who previously enjoyed the prerogatives of nobility.

One of the most suitable means of reinforcing this institution would be to associate the old nobles to it, with prudent reserves and modifications.

I want no other *dukes* than those I create.... If I make a few exceptions for the old nobility, these exceptions will be very limited and apply only to historic names that are useful to preserve....

The old nobles I want in the new institution must all have retained their fortune.

To avoid misunderstanding and have a clear idea of what remains of the old noble caste, we can divide it into three classes:

1) Those employed [by the government];

2) Those with distinguished names but no fortune, who merit being raised from obscurity and misery;

3) Those whom we should definitively eliminate, such as non-amnestied emigrés and those still attached to the Princes of the former dynasty.

The first class should be subdivided.

We will take the old nobles who were attached to the Court ... such as *Chamberlains* and *Ecuyers*, most of whom have fortune and a

---

Archives Nationales, AF IV 1310. Emphases in original.

name. We will give them a title which will become hereditary with the institution of an entailment.

In the second class should be placed those [who exercised public authority], whether administrative or judiciary.... From this large number of functionaries, most of whom are rich and influential, it should be easy to choose 400–500 who, being admitted into the new institution, will help solidify and propagate it....

Applied to an additional 400–500 people, this favor will result in about 1,000 families who will contract new engagements toward the state....

It would be best not to give an individual the same title he had under the Old Regime.... The plan whose elements I have just indicated will be applied with even greater latitude to Piedmont, Tuscany, and Rome. In these countries, few people have served [the state], but there are people with distinguished names whom we must associate with the new institution in order to destroy old memories.

5

An Age of War

Total War

37

CARL VON CLAUSEWITZ

On War

1832

The following is an excerpt from Prussian military philosopher Carl von Clausewitz's (1780–1831) posthumously published work on military strategy, On War. *In it, the veteran of the Napoleonic Wars discusses how the French Revolution and Napoleon changed the nature of warfare, ushering in a new age of "total war."*

Austria and Prussia tried to meet [the French Revolution] with the diplomatic type of war that we have described. They soon discovered its inadequacy. Looking at the situation in this conventional manner, people at first expected to have to deal only with a seriously weakened French army; but in 1793 a force appeared that beggared all imagination. Suddenly war again became the business of the people—a

---

Carl von Clausewitz, *On War*, ed. and trans. Michael Howard and Peter Paret (Princeton, N.J.: Princeton University Press, 1976), 591–93.

people of thirty millions, all of whom considered themselves to be citizens. . . . The people became a participant in war; instead of governments and armies as heretofore, the full weight of the nation was thrown into the balance. The resources and efforts now available for use surpassed all conventional limits; nothing now impeded the vigor with which war could be waged, and consequently the opponents of France faced the utmost peril.

The effects of this innovation did not become evident or fully felt until the end of the revolutionary wars. The revolutionary quarrels did not yet advance inevitably toward the ultimate conclusion: the destruction of the European monarchies. Here and there the German armies were still able to resist them and stem the tide of victory. But all this was really due only to technical imperfections that hampered the French, and which became evident first in the rank and file, then in their generals, and under the Directory in the government itself.

Once these imperfections were corrected by Bonaparte, this juggernaut of war, based on the strength of the entire people, began its pulverizing course through Europe. It moved with such confidence and certainty that whenever it was opposed by armies of the traditional type there could never be a moment's doubt as to the result. Just in time, the reaction set in. The Spanish War spontaneously became the concern of the people. In 1809 the Austrian government made an unprecedented effort with reserves and militia; it came within sight of success and far surpassed everything Austria had earlier considered possible. In 1812 Russia took Spain and Austria as models: her immense spaces permitted her measures—belated though they were—to take effect, and even increased their effectiveness. The result was brilliant. In Germany, Prussia was first to rise. She made the war a concern of the people, and with half her former population, without money or credit, she mobilized a force twice as large as she had in 1806. Little by little the rest of Germany followed her example, and Austria too—though her effort did not equal that of 1809—exerted an exceptional degree of energy. The result was that in 1813 and 1814 Germany and Russia put about a million men into the field against France—counting all who fought and fell in the two campaigns.

Under these conditions the war was waged with a very different degree of vigor. Although it did not always match the intensity of the French, and was at times even marked by timidity, campaigns were on the whole conducted in the new manner, not in that of the past. In the space of only eight months the theater of operations changed from the Oder to the Seine. Proud Paris had for the first time to bow her head, and the terrible Bonaparte lay bound and chained.

Since Bonaparte, then, war, first among the French and subsequently among their enemies, again became the concern of the people as a whole, took on an entirely different character, or rather closely approached its true character, its absolute perfection. There seemed no end to the resources mobilized; all limits disappeared in the vigor and enthusiasm shown by governments and their subjects. Various factors powerfully increased that vigor: the vastness of available resources, the ample field of opportunity, and the depth of feeling generally aroused. The sole aim of war was to overthrow the opponent. Not until he was prostrate was it considered possible to pause and try to reconcile the opposing interests.

War, untrammeled by any conventional restraints, had broken loose in all its elemental fury. This was due to the peoples' new share in these great affairs of state; and their participation, in turn, resulted partly from the impact that the Revolution had on the internal conditions of every state and partly from the danger that France posed to everyone.

Will this always be the case in the future? ... Or shall we again see a gradual separation taking place between government and people? Such questions are difficult to answer, and we are the last to dare to do so. But the reader will agree with us when we say that once barriers—which in a sense consist only in man's ignorance of what is possible—are torn down, they are not so easily set up again.

The Mud and Majesty of War

38

FRANÇOIS-RENÉ CAILLOUX (POUGET)

Napoleon Decorating His Troops

1895

During Napoleon's fifteen years in power, France was at peace only once, during the uneasy, fourteen-month truce known as the Peace of Amiens (March 1802–May 1803). War was the normal state of affairs during his rule. Its effects spread outward from the battlefields and the armies to civil society. Some believed that warfare was a glorious, elevating enterprise that bred a military spirit in nations. But war on a Napoleonic scale also provoked resentment of, and resistance to, its unprecedented demands in material resources and human life. We begin with the armies, with an officer's description of Napoleon's habit of personally decorating soldiers who had distinguished themselves in battle.

Before breaking camp, we were told that the Emperor would review us; we knew not why. We were in formation, my regiment on the right, when we saw him coming at 10 AM. When His Majesty dismounted, he asked me which sapper had struck the first [axe] blow to the castle door; I named him. "Have him step forward." It was Corporal Hattin. . . . "You are a brave man, I give you the cross." "Have your battalion commanders come forward," the Emperor said. When they were there, His Majesty asked me for the bravest officer of the regiment. Unprepared for this question, I hesitated. "Well, did you hear me?" "Yes, Sire, but I know many who . . ." "No waffling, answer." I named lieutenant Guyot, who had been stationed as a marksman at the castle entrance and had remained there, fearless, although exposed to the greatest peril. The Emperor looked at the battalion

François-René Cailloux dit Pouget, *Souvenirs de guerre (1790–1831)* (Paris: La Vouivre, 1998), 135.

commanders and asked them: "Do you agree, messieurs?" "Yes, Sire." "Have that officer come here." He arrived, greatly moved, unaware why he was being summoned. "Your superiors designate you as the bravest officer of the regiment; I name you baron and give you 4,000 livres annually as an entailment." This officer would have been less pale and shaken if he had just heard his death sentence. The Emperor spoke again: "Who is the regiment's bravest soldier?" This question was even more uncomfortable for me. A battalion commander came to my rescue, saying: "Colonel, what about carabineer Bayonnette?" "Is that your opinion, messieurs?" asked the Emperor. "Yes, Sire." "Have him come." This name greatly pleased [the Emperor], who repeated it several times before the soldier arrived. "You are the regiment's bravest soldier," he said. "I name you knight of the Legion of Honor and add to the title a 1,500-franc endowment you can transmit to your children."

It is impossible to describe the effect of these nominations . . . on the whole regiment, from the colonel to the simple soldiers.

39

JEAN-BAPTISTE-ANTOINE-MARCELIN MARBOT

The Battle of Austerlitz

1891

The following account of the climax of the Battle of Austerlitz, from the memoirs of Jean-Baptiste-Antoine-Marcelin Marbot (1782–1854), offers a soldier's view of what, as an old man, he remembered as the horrible majesty of war.

Marshal Soult took the village of Pratzen and the immense plateau of the same name which commanded the entire countryside and, consequently, the battlefield. There, before the Emperor, occurred ex-

Jean-Baptiste-Antoine-Marcelin Marbot, *Mémoires du général baron de Marbot*, vol. 1 (Paris: Plon, 1891), 260–63.

tremely violent combat in which the Russians were beaten. But a battalion of the 4th of the line, whose colonel was Napoleon's brother
Prince Joseph, having pursued the enemy too far, was charged and
pierced by the knight-guards and heavy cavalry of Grand-Duke Con-
stantin, brother of [Emperor] Alexander, who captured its eagle! . . .
Waves of Russian cavalry advanced rapidly to exploit the knight-
guards' momentary success; but Napoleon, having launched against
them the Mamelukes,[1] light horse, and horse grenadiers of his Guard,
led by Marshal Bessières and General Rapp, an extremely bloody
melee occurred. The Russian squadrons were broken and thrown
back beyond Austerlitz village with huge losses. Our cavalry captured
many standards and prisoners, including Prince Repnine, commander
of the knight-guards. This regiment, composed of the most brilliant
young Russian nobility, took heavy losses, because their [tactics] were
known to our soldiers [who] . . . fell upon them, yelling, while they ran
them through with sabers: "Let's make the St. Petersburg ladies
weep!" . . .

From this moment, the heavy Austro-Russian masses . . . were
caught in a crossfire and fell into an incredible state of confusion; their
ranks got muddled and everyone tried to flee. Some ran pell-mell into
the swamps . . . but our infantry pursued them; others tried to escape
by the path between the two lakes, but our cavalry charged and
effected a frightful butchery; finally, the majority, mainly Russians,
sought to escape over the frozen lakes. [The ice] was very thick, and
already 5–6,000 men, who had kept some order, had reached the
middle of the lake . . . when Napoleon, calling the artillery of his
Guard, ordered it to fire cannonballs onto the ice. It broke at many
points, and a great cracking was heard! . . . We saw thousands of Russians, horses, cannons, and wagons, slowly sink into the abyss! . . . A
horribly majestic spectacle I will never forget!

---

[1]Modeled on the Egyptian Mamelukes, this elite cavalry unit was part of Napoleon's
personal guard.

40

ALFRED DE VIGNY

Military Grandeur

1835

The following document is excerpted from the recollections of writer Alfred de Vigny (1797–1863). A schoolboy during the final years of the empire, Vigny dreamed of military glory and became an officer in 1814, as soon as he was old enough. But it was too late to take part in the Napoleonic adventure. After twenty years spent as an undistinguished junior officer in a succession of garrison towns, Vigny exchanged his sword for a pen. His testimony suggests how deeply the cult of military glory could penetrate civilian society and what a profound mark it could leave.

Born with the century, I belong to the generation which, suckled on Imperial bulletins, always had before its eyes a naked sword and went to grasp it at the very moment when France returned it to the Bourbon scabbard. . . . One cannot always play the role one would have liked. . . . As I write [1835], veterans with 20 years' service have not seen pitched battle. I have few adventures to recount, but I have heard many. . . .

Toward the Empire's end, I was a distracted schoolboy. War was afoot in the school, the drum drowned out our teachers, and the mysterious voice of books spoke a cold and pedantic language. To us, logarithms and tropes were just steps we had to climb while ascending to the star of the Legion of Honor, the most beautiful in heaven for children.

With our heads constantly spinning from the roar of cannons and the bells of Te Deums, studies could not hold our attention! When one of our brothers, who had left school several months before, reap-

---

Alfred de Vigny, *Servitude et grandeur militaires* (1835; repr., Paris: Gallimard, 1992), 31–37.

peared in a hussar uniform, his arm in a sling, we felt embarrassed at our books and threw them at our teachers' heads. Even the teachers constantly read us bulletins from the Grand Army, and our cries of "Long Live the Emperor!" interrupted Tacitus and Plato. Our teachers resembled heralds-at-arms, our classrooms barracks, our recreation maneuvers, and our exams reviews.

I was seized by a truly wild love for the glory of arms, a passion all the more unfortunate because it was exactly the time, as I said, when France was beginning to get over it. But the storm still raged, and neither my severe, unrefined, forced, and premature studies, nor the bustle of the wide world . . . could remove this obsession. . . .

Only much later I realized my services were nothing but a long mistake, and that I had brought to an entirely active life a completely contemplative nature. But I followed the inclination of that generation of Empire, born with the century, and to which I belonged.

To us, war seemed so much the natural state of our country that, having finally escaped from school, we threw ourselves into the army. . . .

41

PIERRE-FRANÇOIS PERCY

Campaign Journal
1806

This extract from the campaign diary of Pierre-François Percy (1754–1827), chief surgeon of the Grand Army, offers a very different view of war than that imagined by Vigny and his schoolboy companions. Perhaps even more than the appalling conditions, what struck Percy about Poland in the winter of 1806 was the mud.

Pierre-François Percy, *Journal des campagnes du baron Percy, chirurgien en chef de la Grande Armée* (Paris: Plon, 1904), 133–37.

DECEMBER 26–28, 1806

It was cold and windy. There we were in a little cart; we progressed, but after having gone half a league, we found the heavy cavalry regiment proceeding slowly in single file because of the unsure footing. We tried to cut across the fields: many coaches got stuck; ours barely got out, and the path got even worse. I then decided to ride on horseback and send the poor coachmen back to the village we had just left. I rode through an irresistible wind mixed with hail and snow. Everywhere we saw the debris of carts, horses buried in the mud and unable to get out, cows dying, stuck in the ground up to their stomachs. Here, one of yesterday's battlefields; happily there were only a few cadavers. There, houses were burning; we passed behind them to avoid being suffocated by the smoke. The only sounds here drove man and beast to redouble their efforts to escape this godforsaken terrain, where the so-called road had disappeared beneath water and mud. His Majesty's six-wheeled carriages have suffered the same fate as the rest; the wheels sink in horrible mud holes and the superb, white team, having fallen into and rolled in the mire, was soon unrecognizable. . . .

The French army has never been worse off. The soldier, always on the march, bivouacking every night, spending each day in mud up to his ankles, has not an ounce of bread, not a drop of spirits, no time to dry his clothes, and collapses from fatigue and starvation. There are some who drop dead on the edge of the roadside ditches; a glass of wine or brandy would save them.

The Civilian Experience of War

42

FRIEDRICH LUDWIG BURK

Diary

1813

The impact of war reached deep into the world of civilians. One of the most common ways in which Europeans felt its presence was through the depredations of passing soldiers. Although few areas were spared, central Europe was the principal theater of the Napoleonic wars and thus the area that experienced most directly the burdens of billeting, foraging, and occupation. The following document is an excerpt from the diary of Friedrich Ludwig Burk, a relatively prosperous farmer in Wiesbaden, Germany. In the path of the French retreat after their defeat at the Battle of Leipzig (October 16–19, 1813), his village had to host large detachments of the fleeing French and pursuing allied armies.

OCTOBER 29, 1813

The French are now in full retreat. We don't notice it too much here, but from Frankfurt all the way to Hochheim and Mainz the streets are teeming with them. This week straggling regiments, some unarmed and others without horses, passed through. . . .

NOVEMBER 2, 1813

The last French we had to billet left. We survived their retreat without too much hardship.

NOVEMBER 4, 1813

Around 11:00 AM, the first Cossacks, five to six of them, came through the town . . . and continued through to Bierstadt. One of them

Das Tagebuch des Friedrich Ludwig Burk, ed. Jochen Dollwet and Thomas Weichel (Wiesbaden: Schriften des Stadtsarchivs Wiesbaden, 1993), 72–77. Translation by Claudia Liebeskind.

was shot dead by the French. Austrian Hussars and Uhlans, together with some Tyrolian Jaegers, arrived in the afternoon. Several hundred men spent the night in and around Mossbach.

NOVEMBER 5, 1813

Five thousand Cossacks arrived and set up camp outside town. . . . Bread and brandy, wood and forage, were brought to them. In addition, they took a lot of wood, beanpoles, tree trunks, and kindling from the town and its environs, built themselves straw huts, and stayed the night.

NOVEMBER 14, 1813

Already by the 14th, my mother had to deliver [to the Cossacks] twenty-seven hundredweights of hay and fifty-six bales of straw. On the 11th, the entire Cossack corps arrived. The whole town was full of them. There were horses tied up in every house and shed, and even on the streets at bakeries where they had to be fed by the shopkeepers. There were straw huts erected in the marketplace, huge fires burning, people cooking, whole rows of horses tied up there and being fed. The fields just outside town . . . were even more full of Cossacks, with whole lanes of straw huts. Hay and straw, bread and livestock, were brought to them there.

NOVEMBER 17, 1813

The Prussians appeared on the 15th, but the Cossacks, who were supposed to move on, remained. Because they did not receive any more food and forage, they helped themselves from the surrounding villages: hay, grain, and straw, cattle and sheep, indeed everything they could find. They even cut down all the saplings which lined the road to Erbenheim. More and more Prussians arrived, and on the 17th the Cossacks finally moved on to Frankfurt. The state of their encampment was indescribable. It was strewn with dead and half-dead horses, the intestines and hides of slaughtered livestock, pitchers, bottles, and pots of butter, cheese, plum butter, honey, beehives, flour, apples, nuts, whole heaps of spoiled hay, bunches of fruit, ladders, crockery and firewood, poles, sheepskins, whole and cut up sack that they had received full of oats, dried meats — all taken from our region. On leaving, they burned their straw huts.

NOVEMBER 22, 1813

The town is now full of Prussians; my mother has 16 of them billeted on her. Up to now, she has had to furnish 30-and-a-half hundredweights of hay. The town council searched for oats in the attic, and she had to turn over one more big sack.

NOVEMBER 24, 1813

She now has 24 Prussians billeted on her, and often an additional six to eight show up at night.

NOVEMBER 25, 1813

Had to deliver hay, straw, oats; those who had no oats had to give grain. Our duke had to provide auxiliary troops.

NOVEMBER 30, 1813

My brother Joh[ann] Heinrich was summoned for militia service with his company; this brought my mother great sorrow.

DECEMBER 1, 1813

The whole house is full of soldiers, the stables of horses. Tonight there were another five Prussian Uhlan horses tied up in the courtyard. Requisitions continue. Many people are lying ill, suffering from a nervous illness called lazaret fever.

DECEMBER 19, 1813

On the 14th, my brother Joh[ann] Friederich fell seriously ill. Many people are dying now. On the 15th my mother's sister died and on the 19th, her husband; both their children, Conrad and his sister, are very ill. I have not removed my clothes for eight days and have not gotten into bed because of all the upheaval.

DECEMBER 31, 1813

It is crawling with Prussians and Russians. From the 30th to the 31st, they marched through the town all day and all night to go to Braubach where they were to cross the Rhine. None of us will forget this year. Whoever has not experienced it personally would not believe the hardship war brings. Thousands dead on the battlefield, thousands crippled, and thousands more, in poverty, misfortune, and misery, who go to an early grave. It is impossible to describe all the misery of war.

This year, everything grew well, especially the potatoes, turnips, and edible roots.

43

NAPOLEON BONAPARTE

On Conscription

undated

The empire itself was largely spared the hardships described in the previous document, at least until 1814. But it had to bear another burden, the burden of conscription. Napoleon's military endeavors demanded a constant supply of recruits to replenish the ever-diminishing ranks of his armies. With as many as 960,000 conscripts called up in one year (1813), the human demands of Napoleonic warfare could not be met by volunteerism. Consequently, Napoleon maintained and honed the system of conscription he had inherited from the Revolution. Conscription was probably the most unpopular institution of his regime. Nonetheless, Napoleon hoped that, with time, the obligation to perform military service would become an honored civic rite of passage. In this excerpt from a discussion he had during his captivity on Saint Helena, Napoleon elaborates on his dream.

[Conscription] made the French army the best-composed in history. It was an eminently national institution and was already well-entrenched in our mores; only mothers still complained about it. The time would have come when a girl would not have wanted a boy who had not acquitted his debt to the fatherland. It is at that point alone that conscription would have reached its maximum usefulness. When it no longer seems like a punishment or forced labor, when it becomes a point of pride . . . it is only then that a nation is grand, glorious, strong; then it can face defeats, invasions, centuries.

Emmanuel-Auguste, comte de Las Cases, *Mémoires de Napoléon Ier (Mémorial de Sainte-Hélène)*, vol. 4 (Paris: Cocuaud, n.d.), 53–54.

44

Song of Vivarais Conscripts

1810

The public's actual attitude toward conscription bore little resemblance to Napoleon's hopeful vision. In reality, administrators were happy if they obtained resigned, if sullen, compliance with their seemingly endless demands for fresh recruits. The following document, a poem written by several conscripts departing for the armies, suggests the emotions conscription aroused in those it called.

I am a poor conscript
Of the year 1810
I must leave Languedoc
Languedoc, Languedoc, Oh!
I must leave Languedoc
With a pack upon my back

The mayor and the prefect too
Are just government lackeys
They make us draw straws
Draw straws, draw straws
They make us draw straws
To send us to our deaths

So goodbye dear parents
Don't forget your child
Write him from time to time
From time to time, from time to time
Write him from time to time
To send him money

So goodbye dear pretties
Who have bewitched our hearts

M. Chaulanges, A. G. Manry, and R. Sève, *Textes historiques, 1799–1815: L'époque de Napoléon* (Paris: Delagrave, 1960), 102.

Don't cry when we leave
When we leave, when we leave
Don't cry when we leave
We'll come back sooner or later

So goodbye my dear heart
You will console my sister
You will tell her that Fanfan[1]
That Fanfan, that Fanfan
Was killed in battle

Those who wrote this song
Are only three fine boys
They were stocking makers
Stocking makers, stocking makers
And now they are soldiers.

[1] *Fanfan*: Nickname for François.

45

Replacement Contract

March 27, 1809

Some young men could legally avoid conscription. These were the sons of wealthy families who could afford a replacement for their sons. Under the replacement system, draftees could escape conscription by paying others to serve in their stead. Thousands of well-to-do young men availed themselves of this opportunity, paying impecunious young men to take their place. Replacement agreements were formalized before notaries and registered with the government. The following document is a typical replacement contract. It is worth noting that this particular replacement took advantage of his presence before the local notary to have a last will and testament drawn up. It was witnessed by the father and son who had just purchased his service.

Archives Départementales de l'Hérault, 2 E 14, 470.

... Were present François Belpel, landowner at Portirargues, currently living in Agde, ... acting for Antoine-François-Louis Belpel, his son, and Jacques-Pierre-Esprit Aoust [son of a Béziers chair-turner]. ...

1) Jacques-Pierre-Esprit Aoust, ... of his own free will, agrees to replace Antoine-François-Louis Belpel in military service ... and to that effect promises to present himself at the first summons and without delay to the responsible civil and military authorities, to have his replacement validated, to receive his marching orders and then proceed to his designated corps.

2) The parties agree that the price of the present replacement will be 4,600 francs, of which François Belpel, the father, has counted out and given 1,400 to Aoust, who verified it and received it before myself and witnesses. Belpel promises to pay the remaining 3,200 francs to Aoust upon his discharge, ... provided that his son is not asked to furnish another replacement, or to pay it to his heirs if he dies during his military service. ... It is also stipulated that, until the 3,200 francs have been paid, Belpel will pay 5% interest on this sum, in bi-annual payments.

3) If this replacement is not accepted, if Jacques-Pierre-Esprit Aoust deserts within two years, or if Belpel, the son, is forced to serve in person or to furnish another replacement the present contract will be considered null and void, and Belpel will have the right to recover the sum of 1,400 francs and any interest he may have paid.

4) To guarantee the obligations Belpel has contracted, he assigns and mortgages the buildings, fields, and vineyards he owns in the commune of Portirargues; and for his part, Aoust, having no personal property, assigns and mortgages what he may acquire in the future. ...

46

MAYOR OF ROQUEBRUNE

Letter to the Prefect of the Hérault
October 10, 1805

Most able-bodied conscripts could not afford a replacement; for them, the choice was between compliance and resistance. Draft resistance was widespread and took many forms: refusing to obey the initial summons, faking a disqualifying ailment or inflicting a real injury on oneself, contracting a simulated marriage, hiding in nearby hills or forests and living on the charity of family and friends, fleeing to another part of the country, or deserting while en route to the armies. The government employed different means to combat draft resistance. At first it relied on the persuasive power of local officials, particularly mayors, to secure compliance. In the following letter, a small-town mayor voices his frustration at his failure to persuade his fellow citizens to cooperate.

In my letter of the 3rd of this month, I related all I've done to get this town's draft resisters to appear for duty. I wrote that only a few of them agreed. I had the pleasure of seeing nine others join them. . . . This little troop left for Béziers the 5th of the month [and] . . . went on to Montpellier the following day. Several days later, I was told that others were inclined to follow their example. I was thrilled by this news, which gave me hope that all would soon depart [for the army]. But . . . I have just learned that, with one exception, all have returned.

My hopes have been completely dashed; I had convinced myself that the example given by the nine conscripts would encourage the others; that the letters they wrote from Montpellier would greatly help my efforts. But at the very moment when I thought I could use them as a good example, word of their desertion killed the good dispositions beginning to take root in those who had remained behind.

Archives Départementales de l'Hérault, 2R 811, Mayor Sabatier of Roquebrune to the Prefect of the Hérault.

I nonetheless tried [to change their minds] by reading them the attached proclamation. . . . Nothing is sadder than the position of a man who wants only good, who desires it, who tries everything to attain it, but has no other means than his feeble voice. . . .

Proclamation

Conscripts, will you remain indifferent to honor's call? Will you remain deaf to the fatherland's cry? Will you ignore the law which orders you to leave your homes for a post on the frontiers? Have you not heard, or have you pretended not to hear, my most recent proclamation in which I announced that His Imperial and Royal Majesty agreed to overlook your faults if you renounced the perverse sentiments that led you to commit them? Can only punishment make you understand your true interests? Do you find it more glorious to be condemned to pay fines and rot in prison than to be counted in the new battalions destined to win laurels on the field of honor?

Conscripts, come to your senses. The law will have its way; yes, you will do as it commands or be punished. . . .

Parents of conscripts, do you love your children? Get them to depart; your ruin is inevitable if they do not take this course.

Parents of conscripts, and all my fellow citizens, I do not tire of repeating that you must give neither shelter nor work to conscripts called to the service of the fatherland. Innkeepers, cabaret-owners, you must give them nothing to eat at the risk of a very heavy fine and a year's imprisonment.

47

SUBPREFECT OF THE HAUTE-LOIRE

Letter to the Prefect

February 12, 1811

Over the years, the regime adopted more coercive measures to enforce compliance with conscription. These included billeting soldiers in the homes of draft resisters and forcing the wealthiest villagers to foot the bill, as well as dispatching troops to root out draft evaders. By 1811 the regime had made tangible progress in obtaining compliance. Nonetheless, large-scale resistance remained a problem in many areas. The following letter from the subprefect of the Haute-Loire to his superior, the prefect, describes the persistence of resistance and reflects on its causes.

I am as troubled as you by the sustained resistance of the resisters, procrastinators, and deserters of my district. I have tried everything to overcome it. . . . The contingents were furnished with the greatest difficulty, it is true, but finally they were, and that has never happened before. The spirit of the district has clearly improved and there is reason to hope for further progress.

Yet, it still contains many resisters, procrastinators, and deserters who persist in a nearly invincible disobedience that requires the most vigorous measures. . . .

Their opposition and repugnance have been strengthened by perfidious sermons and insinuations from the time when there were counterrevolutionary camps and parties.

In those troubled times, young men who joined the armies were the subject of anathemas and eternal damnation; those who appeared in military uniform were assassinated in cold blood; those who were spared were covered with opprobrium and ridicule; those killed on the field of honor were refused funeral services; religious fanatics . . . brought food and ammunition to draft dodgers and insurgent desert-

---

M. Chaulanges, A. G. Manry, and R. Sève, *Textes historiques, 1799–1815: L'époque de Napoléon* (Paris: Delagrave, 1960), 103–5.

ers in the lairs and caverns where they were hiding and encouraged them to revolt. . . .

Almost all the priests who then preached insurrection are still in the same parishes. . . .

It is difficult, if not impossible, to reach most of the resisters, as they have no property and are hired by wealthy proprietors in [neighboring] departments. . . .

The exemptions purchased by healthy and wealthy conscripts embitter and exasperate the poor who have been summoned to take their place and have infinitely increased or served as pretext for their resistance.

. . . Unfortunately [this climate of opinion] also affects a number of mayors, their deputies, and municipal councils; without having any illegalities to report, I wish to complain of their lack of courage; one would say that they are afraid of public opinion and are afraid to commit themselves openly to pursuing resisters and deserters. . . . Neither taste nor opinion are favorable to conscription.

The Moral Impact of War

48

BENJAMIN CONSTANT

On the Spirit of Conquest
1814

The Napoleonic Wars took a greater toll in human life and material resources than had any previous European conflict. One incisive contemporary observer, Benjamin Constant, believed that the impact of the Napoleonic Wars on political culture and public morality was even greater. In 1814 Constant published On the Spirit of Conquest, *a study of war's subtle, corrupting influence on the soul of a conquering nation.*

Benjamin Constant, *Oeuvres* (Paris: Gallimard, 1957), 969–72.

The following is an extract from Chapter 8, "The Effects of a Conquering Government on the Mass of the Nation."

A government given over to the spirit of invasion and conquest would corrupt some of the people [the military], making them serve actively in its enterprises. While corrupting that chosen portion, it would also act upon the rest of the nation, whose passive obedience and sacrifices it demanded, so as to hinder its rationality, distort its judgment, and upset its ideas.

When a people is naturally warlike, the dominant authority need not fool it in order to take it to war. Attila simply pointed out to his Huns the part of the world on which they were to descend, and they fell upon it, because Attila was but the instrument and representative of their underlying drive. But today, as war brings no advantages to the people and is only a source of privation and suffering, the justification for a system of conquest must rely on sophisms and imposture. . . .

The government would never dare say to the nation: Let us march to conquer the world. The nation would respond unanimously: we do not want to conquer the world.

The government would speak instead of national independence, national honor, the straightening of its frontiers, commercial interests, necessary precautions; and even more I cannot imagine because the vocabulary of hypocrisy and injustice is inexhaustible.

It would speak of national independence as if the independence of the nation was compromised by other nations' independence.

It would speak of national honor, as if national honor would suffer if other nations kept their honor.

It would allege the need to straighten frontiers, as if that doctrine, once admitted, would not banish forever from the earth all peace and equity. It is always toward the exterior that a government seeks to round out its frontiers. As far as I know, none has ever relinquished a portion of its territory to give to the rest greater geometric regularity. Thus, the straightening of frontiers is a system that defeats itself, whose elements contradict one another, and whose execution, requiring the spoliation of the weak, renders illegitimate the possession of the strong.

The government would invoke commercial interests, as if it helped the economy to depopulate a country of its youth, deprive it of those most necessary to agriculture, manufacturing, and industry, and raise bloody barriers between itself and foreign peoples. Commerce rests on good understanding between nations; it is sustained only by justice; it is founded on equality; it prospers in peace; and it would be in the interest of commerce that a government would ceaselessly reignite bitter wars, that it would summon upon its own people universal hatred, that it would perpetuate injustice after injustice, that it would continually undermine its credit by violence, that it would not tolerate equals!

Under the pretext of precautions required by prudence and foresight, the government would attack its most peaceful neighbors, its most humble allies, in attributing to them hostile intentions and claiming to preempt acts of aggression. If the unfortunate objects of its calumnies were easily subjugated, it would boast about having thwarted their plans; if they had the time and force to resist, they would say, you see, they wanted war because they are defending themselves. . . .

The authorities would thus have to undertake, on the intellectual faculties of the mass of its subjects, the same work as on the moral qualities of the military. They would have to try to banish all logic from the minds of the former, as it would have to try to stifle all humanity in the hearts of the latter: words would lose their meaning; moderation would herald violence; justice would announce iniquity. The right of nations would become a code of expropriation and barbarity: all the notions that the wisdom of the past several centuries has introduced into the relations between societies and individuals would be abandoned. The human race would sink back toward those times of devastation that were the disgrace of history. The only difference would be hypocrisy; and this hypocrisy would be even more corrupting since no one would believe it. The lies of authority are not only dangerous when they fool and mislead the people; they are no less so when they fool no one.

Subjects who suspect their masters of duplicity and perfidiousness themselves acquire the habit of perfidiousness and duplicity: he who hears the head of government called a great politician because every line he writes is an imposture, in his turn wants to be a great politician in his subaltern sphere; truth seems to him inanity, fraud cleverness. He used to lie out of self-interest; he will now lie out of self-love as well. He will have the self-deceit of treachery; and if that contagion infects an essentially imitative people, a people who fears more than anything else to appear as dupes, can private morality avoid being engulfed in the shipwreck of public morality?

6

Napoleon and Europe

The Liberator

49

NAPOLEON BONAPARTE

On Europe

undated

By the end of 1810, Napoleon ruled over an empire of 44 million inhabitants. In addition to the French, the empire included millions of Flemings, Germans, Italians, and even Croatians. Bordering the empire were satellite kingdoms—Holland, Westphalia, and Naples—ruled by family members. These lands were forced to bear much of the burden of Napoleon's war effort. Yet his European legacy was not entirely negative. French laws and institutions were applied to these areas. Feudalism was replaced with a modern property regime, archaic administrative structures with streamlined Napoleonic ones, and customary law with the Civil Code. The very creation of satellite kingdoms and allied states like the Confederation of the Rhine consolidated patchwork polities descended from the Middle Ages into more uniform, national units. In the following statement, delivered after his fall from power, Napoleon defends his European legacy.

Emmanuel-Auguste, comte de Las Cases, *Mémoires de Napoléon Ier (Mémorial de Sainte-Hélène)*, Vol. 16 (Paris: Cocuaud, n.d.), 94–96.

One of my grand thoughts was the agglomeration, the concentration of the same geographic peoples that revolution and politics had dissolved and fragmented. Although scattered, there are in Europe 30 million French, 15 million Spaniards, 15 million Italians, 30 million Germans: I would have liked to make each of these peoples a single, compact nation. With such a cortege, it would have been magnificent to move forward for posterity, with the blessing of centuries to come. I felt myself worthy of that glory!

After this brief simplification . . . it would have been possible to realize the beautiful, but elusive ideal of civilization; in this state of affairs, we would have had a better chance of establishing uniform laws, principles, opinions, sentiments, views, and interests. Then perhaps, thanks to the spread of enlightenment, it would have become possible to apply to the great European family [the model of] the American Congress or the assemblies of Greece; and then what a perspective of force, grandeur, enjoyment, prosperity! What a grand and magnificent spectacle! . . .

The agglomeration of 30 or 40 million French had already been perfected; that of 15 million Spaniards was almost at the same point. . . . Three or four years [of Napoleonic rule] would have produced a profound peace, a brilliant posterity, a compact nation, and I would have earned their thanks; I would have spared them the frightful tyranny that oppresses them, the terrible disturbances that await them.

As for the 15 million Italians, their consolidation was already well advanced; it only had to solidify with age, and each day unifying their principles and legislation, their thought and feeling, that infallible, guaranteed cement of human communities. The union of Piedmont to France, that of Parma, Tuscany, Rome, was only temporary in my thinking, and had no purpose but to oversee, guarantee, and further the Italians' national education. . . .

German unification had to go slower; thus, all I did was simplify their monstrous complication; it is not that they were unprepared for centralization: to the contrary, they were too much so, they would have followed us blindly. . . . How can it be that no German prince has understood his nation's predisposition and how to exploit it? Assuredly, if heaven had made me a German prince, . . . I would have certainly governed 30 million united Germans; and, from what I know of them, I still think that, if they had ever elected me . . . they would have never abandoned me and I would not be here [Saint Helena]. . . .

Whatever happens, this consolidation will take place sooner or later. . . . I have set it in motion, and I think that after my fall and the disappearance of my system, there is no other grand equilibrium possible than the unification and confederation of the great peoples. The first sovereign who . . . will embrace in good faith the cause of nations, will find himself at the head of all Europe and will be able to attempt anything.

50

MATHIEU-LOUIS MOLÉ

Opening Discourse to the Assembly of the Jews

1806

Napoleon is still remembered in parts of Europe as the man who eman- cipated the Jews. The conquests of the French revolutionary and Napo- leonic armies brought many central European Jews into the empire. Although the Jews of France had received full citizenship in 1791, those of the newly incorporated areas had not. In 1806 Napoleon decided to regulate their status. He summoned an assembly of European Jewish leaders to answer a series of questions about their relationship to the civil order. The assembly's answers became the basis for regulating relations between Jewish communities and secular authority in the empire. The following document, the discourse of imperial commissioner Mathieu- Louis Molé (1781–1855) presenting the government's questions, reveals the unspoken aims and assumptions behind Napoleon's initiative.

His Majesty the Emperor and King today directs us to inform you of his intentions. None of you ignore the purpose for which His Majesty has summoned you from the four corners of the Empire. You know it; the conduct of many members of your religion provoked complaints that arrived at the foot of the throne; these complaints were well- founded, but, preferring to treat the source of the disease, the Emperor wanted to hear your ideas about how to cure it. You will doubtless prove yourselves worthy of such paternal attention, and you will fully

Diogène Tama, *Collection des actes de l'Assemblée des Israélites de France . . . convoquée à Paris par décret de Sa Majesté impériale et royale du 30 mai 1806* (Paris: 1806), 130–4.

realize the seriousness of the responsibility entrusted to you. Rather than consider the government under which you live as a power against which you have to defend yourselves, you will seek only to enlighten it, to cooperate with it on the improvements it prepares; and thus, by showing that you have learned from the experience of all the French, you will prove that you do not seek to isolate yourselves.

The laws imposed on individuals of your religion have varied across the earth. Momentary considerations have often dictated them. But, just as this assembly has no precedent in the history of Christianity, for the first time you are going to be judged justly, and your destiny will be determined by a Christian prince. His Majesty wants you to be French; it is up to you to accept this title and realize that, if you do not prove yourselves worthy, you renounce it.

We are going to read the questions addressed to you. Your duty is to respond entirely truthfully to each one. We are telling you today, and we will repeat it ceaselessly: when a monarch both firm and just, who knows all, rewards all, and punishes all, questions his subjects, they would reveal both their guilt and blindness to their veritable interests if they did not respond with frankness. . . .

1) Can Jews have multiple wives?
2) Is divorce permitted by the Jewish religion? Is a divorce considered valid without having been decreed by the courts? . . .
3) Can a Jewish woman marry a Christian, a Christian woman a Jewish man? Or does the law require Jews to marry only each other?
4) In the eyes of the Jews, are the French their brothers or foreigners?
5) In either case, what sort of relations does Jewish law prescribe with Frenchmen who are not of their religion?
6) Do Jews born in France and treated by the law as French citizens view France as their fatherland? Are they obliged to defend it? Are they required to obey its laws? . . .
7) Who appoints rabbis?
8) What kind of jurisdiction do rabbis exercise among the Jews? . . .
9) Are the forms of selection [by which rabbis are chosen] and jurisdiction determined by religious laws or only by custom?
10) Does the law of the Jews bar them from certain professions?
11) Does the law of the Jews prevent them from engaging in usury against their brothers?
12) Does it prohibit or permit usury against foreigners?

51

NAPOLEON BONAPARTE

Letter to Jérôme Bonaparte, King of Westphalia
November 15, 1807

Napoleonic domination could mean the introduction of liberal reforms. An example is found in Napoleon's letter to his brother Jérôme (1784–1860), king of Westphalia.

My brother, enclosed you will find your kingdom's constitution.

It contains the conditions under which I renounce all my rights of conquest and all my rights over your country. You should scrupulously observe it. The well-being of your people is important to me, not only because of the influence it can have over your glory and mine, but also over the general European system. Ignore those who tell you that your people, accustomed to servitude, will receive your benefits with gratitude. They are more enlightened in the kingdom of Westphalia than some want you to believe, and your throne can only be truly secured by the confidence and love of the population.

What the people of Germany keenly desire is that talented non-nobles have equal rights to your esteem and to employment; that serfdom and all intermediaries between the sovereign and the lowest class of people be entirely abolished.

The Napoleonic code, judicial transparency, and the establishment of juries will be the distinctive benefits of your rule. . . . I count more on them to extend and firm up your monarchy than on the results of the greatest victories.

Your people must enjoy a degree of liberty, equality, and well-being unknown to the other peoples of Germany. . . . This manner of governing will be a more powerful barrier against Prussia than the Elbe, fortifications, and French protection.

What people would want to return to arbitrary Prussian government once it had tasted the benefits of a wise and liberal administration?

Correspondance de Napoléon, ed. Maximilien Vox (Paris: Gallimard, 1943), 361–62.

The peoples of Germany, France, Italy, and Spain desire equality and want liberal ideas. . . .

Be a constitutional king. If reason and the enlightenment of your century are not enough to convince you, good politics would ordain it, given your position. You will find that you will have the force of public opinion behind you and that you possess a natural ascendancy over your neighbors who are absolute monarchs.

52

NICHOLAS-PHILIBERT DESVERNOIS

Reforms in Naples

1898

The following extract from the memoirs of Nicholas-Philibert Desvernois (1771–1859), aide-de-camp to the war minister of Joseph Bonaparte (1768–1844), king of Naples, summarizes the progressive reforms Joseph implemented there during his brief reign (March 1806–May 1808).

From the seat of truth, the clergy was preaching the eternal principles of the dignity of man.

The suppression of convents and concentration of nuns and monks in pious houses saved much public money.

Feudal judges deemed worthy of the king's confidence received places in the royal judiciary.

Provincial intendants were ordered to employ former monks with the talent and desire to teach; those capable of serving as priests were retained. The most infirm, who had grown old in the cloisters and survived their relatives, were collected in great public establishments.

Scholars who wanted to continue monastic life could devote themselves to study . . . at Monte-Cassino and La Calva: they were given

Nicholas-Philibert Desvernois, *Mémories du général baron Desvernois* (Paris: Plon, 1898), 344–74.

two houses where the libraries and manuscripts of the other religious houses were concentrated.

Other monks, in the establishments of Cinque Miglia and Monte Feruso, modeled on the hospice of Saint Bernard, were to house and care for voyagers in the high, snowy regions of Calabria and Abruzzi. . . .

Each province received a college and a girls' school. The daughters of officers and public functionaries had a central house at Aversa specially supervised by the Queen. . . .

Roads were opened from Naples to Reggio; the provincial administration, and military and civil engineering collaborated on them. Thus was a centuries-old project completed. . . .

Artillery commander, General Devon, established several arms workshops at Annonciade and foundries at Mongiana. . . .

Provincial regiments were created and organized on the French model [and] were generally commanded by the eldest sons of the most important families.

A military school was established under the direction of General Parisi and a topographic bureau organized under the direction of the learned geographer Zannoni. Work on the map of the Kingdom of Naples was resumed and finished. Forts and batteries were repaired; the navy had a battleship, frigates, and 90 gunboats. . . .

Two thousand vagrants were organized into a corps of workers, clothed, fed, and paid. . . . [Through their labor, Naples] was beautified and this part of the population, previously considered incorrigible, became industrious.

Naples, until then lighted only by a few lamps . . . was given streetlights like Paris. . . .

Archaeological excavation was undertaken at Pompeii and Magna Graecia. The academies of Pompeii and Herculaneum were absorbed by the royal academy established by Joseph. . . .

Music conservatories were encouraged; the infamous custom of castration . . . was abolished.

The Academy of painting, also encouraged, soon had 1,200 students. . . .

Direct taxation was abolished, except for a proportional land tax.

The civil list was fixed at 100,000 ducats per month (440,000 francs). Half of this sum was paid in certificates which could be used to acquire national properties. . . .

Public revenues, which under Ferdinand IV were 7,000,000 ducats, were 14,000,000 under Joseph. The debt, which was 100,000,000 under the first of these two monarchs, was halved by Joseph. . . .

Feeling the need to see and hear much, he opened his palace to the nobility, ministers, councilors of State, magistrates, municipal officers of Naples, superior officers of his army. It was in their families that he chose his guests; it is thus that he was able to influence the spirits of all classes of society; it is thus that he made himself loved and cherished by the Neapolitan nation.

53

GIUSEPPE ZURLO

Report on the Abolition of Feudalism in Naples
undated

The most ambitious reform undertaken in the kingdom of Naples by Joseph and his successor, Napoleon's brother-in-law Joachim Murat (1767–1815), was the abolition of feudalism. Yet the commission charged with executing this project encountered enormous difficulties in trying to transform the legal and social framework of landownership in this rural, hierarchical country. When French rule ended in 1815, peasants were still paying dues to their former lords, few common lands had been divided, and little agricultural progress had occurred. In the following document, the head of the feudal commission, Giuseppe Zurlo (1759–1828), reports on progress made and obstacles remaining.

. . . Under feudalism, the Kingdom's population was lagging behind that of other nations which had been exposed to French laws through the arms of the immortal Emperor Napoleon. On August 2, 1806, [you] abolished personal servitude, all jurisdictional rights, monopolies; [you] abolished restrictive water rights, but let the barons keep the lands they possessed as feudal lords. This abstract declaration of what was abolished and retained was not enough to extinguish all that was hateful and burdensome to the people under feudalism. Most feudal rights, which were in the form of dues, were maintained in law,

Carlo Capra, *L'Età Rivoluzionaria e Napoleonica in Italia, 1796–1815* (Turin: Loescher, 1978), 225–59. Translated by Giovanna Sommerfield.

and, for a long time, feudalism seemed to have been abolished only in theory. The centuries-old distinction between feudal lords and the population increased after this law because hopes for improvement were disappointed. . . .

The frictions born of feudalism are coeval to the foundation of the monarchy; no power has been able to extinguish them. The laws have always favored the rights and properties of vassals, but this favor has been rendered useless by government weakness and the jurisdiction exercised by feudal lords.

At the time of the law abolishing feudalism, all previous rights persisted, communal land was held by the barons, communal properties, except for a few, were not recovered, the most unjust arrangements were enforced, villages were crushed by debt and obligatory services. Much feudal land was subject to heavy dues on sowing or harvesting, pasture land remained exclusively in the hands of the barons and caused great damage to agriculture. . . .

The law abolishing feudalism rekindled among the populations hostility toward feudal impositions and led them to desire a government that had justice, strength, and liberality as the foundation of its operations. The august predecessor of Your Majesty had the commendable idea of creating a special commission which would quickly judge all pending controversies, execute the law abolishing feudalism, and limit the power of the barons. But, paralyzed by a series of obstacles, the commission proceeded slowly. It was just beginning its work when Providence gave Your Majesty the throne of Naples. You saw the importance of its operations and perfected them. . . .

Public land emerged from the destruction of private property and, for the opposite reason, one must revive the old division now that all laws favor property and industry. The state properties derive from the feudal system and the large ecclesiastical holdings on which the population had certain rights. Once the inalienability of these properties was removed, it was necessary to retain for the population, . . . all the law allowed. Having recognized the need to multiply properties, to make them free and independent, one could only attain this by parceling out communal property and separating ownership from servitude. . . .

Many possessions were in very bad condition. There was no hope of improvement wherever communal ownership lasted; any private interest could reclaim those plots, and their possession was the cause of disputes. Added to these obstacles were . . . the so-called communal usage rights such as pasturing, woodcutting, acorn-gathering, and other similar, miserable rights. I have mentioned how, under Bourbon rule, the memorable edict of February 23, 1792, was issued to divide and better the common lands; unhappily, nothing came of it. Now the law of September 1, 1806, ordered the division of state properties, of fiefs, churches, commons, and mixed properties, so that they could be owned independently by those among whom they would be divided. . . . But since the law did not define or regulate that division, or estimate the value of the rights for compensation, it remained almost without effect. . . . Another decree was promulgated on June 8, 1807, which determined how to assess state properties. . . . It established that those who acquired state properties were to be absolute owners, able to enclose them or change them in any way, without any interference from communal users. . . .

The division was accompanied by unavoidable inconveniences. . . . In spite of the law, . . . an infinite number of pasture lands remained open, under the pretext that they were necessary to the financial well-being of the communes, as if they could live with a few sheep, as the Bedouins do. . . . Until now, I have not seen anyone take advantage of the decrees of June 20, 1808, and January 17, 1810, to convert feudal service obligations into monetary payments. It was widely believed that it was not permitted to change the form of cultivation without asking the lord, so that . . . I have observed neither agricultural changes nor the redemption of feudal dues, so that many territories in the Kingdom are in the same condition as during feudal times. On the other hand, lands that were supposed to remain intact, like wooded hillsides, were instead cultivated, causing immense damage. Wherever one goes, one sees many places where the abolition of feudalism was in word and not deed.

The Tyrant

54

CHARLES-MAURICE DE TALLEYRAND

Napoleon's European Legacy

1853

Napoleon's European legacy is mixed. Alongside liberal reform came military occupation, heavy taxation, exactions of all kinds, and the ever-present threat of violent repression. Even the most progressive reforms could be perceived as unwanted intrusions, offensive to local customs and threatening to local interests. The following document — Talleyrand's assessment of Napoleon's European policy, in general, and of the impact of Napoleonic rule in Naples and Westphalia, in particular — is sharply at odds with the opinions expressed in documents 50–52.

Everywhere Napoleon provoked hatred and invented difficulties, which, in the long run, became insurmountable. And as if Europe did not furnish him enough, he created new ones, by authorizing the ambitions of his own family. The fatal word he had spoken one day, that before his death his dynasty would be Europe's most ancient, made him give his brothers and his sisters' husbands the thrones and principalities that victory and treachery put into his hands. This is how he disposed of Naples, Westphalia, Holland, Spain, Lucca, even Sweden. . . .

A childish vanity pushed him down this dangerous path. For either these newly created sovereigns respected his overarching plan and became its satellites, which made it impossible for them to take root in the country entrusted to them; or they must reject it. . . . Each new creation thus became a source of dissolution in Napoleon's fortune. We see it everywhere in the last years of his reign. When Napoleon

---

Charles-Maurice de Talleyrand, *Mémoires du Prince de Talleyrand,* vol. 2 (Paris: Henri Javal, 1953), 41–42, 48–50.

gave a crown, he wanted the new king to remain tied to his system of universal domination, to his grand Empire. . . . But no sooner had the one who mounted the throne seized authority, than he wanted to wield it alone and, more or less openly, resisted the hand which sought to subordinate him. Each of these improvised princes believed himself the equal of the most ancient sovereigns of Europe, by the sole fact of a decree and a solemn entry into a capital occupied by a French army corps. The human respect which led them to assert independence made them more dangerous obstacles to Napoleon's ambitions than a natural enemy would have been. Let's follow them for an instant in their royal careers.

I begin with the Kingdom of Naples, which had been conferred (those are the words of the time) on March 30, 1806, to Joseph Bonaparte, the Emperor's older brother. . . .

Within four months, the new king was already quarrelling with his brother. Joseph only resided briefly in Naples; circumstances soon brought him to Spain. During his stay in Naples, power had only been a source of amusement to him. . . . On the throne, he sought only life's pleasures and easy access to libertinism. . . .

Joseph was succeeded by Murat, who was no longer contented by his Grand-Duchy of Berg. No sooner had he crossed the Alps than he dreamed of making himself master of all Italy one day. Under the treaty granting him the throne of Naples, he was obliged to maintain his predecessor's constitution. But, as the administrative provisions of this constitution had not yet been executed, he set aside the reform of civil and criminal law he had promised to undertake, and instead busied himself with completing the country's financial organization. To increase revenue and facilitate tax collection, he began by abolishing all feudal rights. Spurred by his minister Zurlo, he hastened to complete this operation, which he saw only in fiscal terms. And the commission instituted to accomplish it judged all cases pending between lords and villages in favor of the latter; and this took place at the same time as Napoleon was trying to remake aristocracy in France. . . .

The result of this operation was not only to strip the Neapolitan barons of all their feudal rights and dues, but worse, to transfer to the villages most of their lands, which had been undivided for many centuries.

This measure dealt a heavy blow to the nobility's fortunes, but it facilitated tax assessment and brought in more revenue. Thus, within five years, the Neapolitan government raised public revenue from 44 million francs to more than 80 million. . . .

[Overconfident], Murat ordered the French seconded to the Neapolitan service to swear a loyalty oath to him and have themselves naturalized. All were outraged at this demand; and Napoleon, pushed too far, displayed his anger with customary violence. He ordered the French troops in the kingdom to form a camp 12 leagues from Naples; and from this camp, he had a proclamation issued declaring that all French citizens were Neapolitan citizens by right because . . . it was part of the grand Empire.

Murat, who in a moment of passion had let himself be drawn into such an imprudent enterprise, persuaded himself that the Emperor would never pardon him and that he had no choice but to guarantee his security by increasing his power; from this point, he thought only of invading all Italy. The unification to the French Empire of Tuscany, Rome, Holland, and the Hanseatic cities deeply troubled his spirit. The ill-defined use of this word "grand Empire" that he had just heard in the middle of his kingdom completely upset him, and he began to reveal his true views. . . .

[To Westphalia, Jérôme and his advisers] had at first brought from Paris with them a constitution; afterwards they were to adapt to it a judiciary, a military, and a financial system. Their first operation was to divide the territory, and to change thus in a moment without the aid of revolutionary spirit, all the traditions, all the customs, and all the relations that time had established. They then created prefectures, sub-prefectures, and appointed mayors everywhere. They thus transferred into Germany all the machinery of French organization, and pretended to have set it in motion. . . .

The court formed spontaneously; but the budget, raised to the point where the reserves for Napoleon which were composed of half the freehold wealth, forced them to carry it, was for the first years very difficult to establish. This dynasty commenced where the others finished. They were reduced to ad hoc measures from the second year of the reign. They did not seek these expedients in economies that might be made, but in the creation of new taxes. It became necessary, instead of 37 millions of revenue, which would have been sufficient to furnish the necessary expenses of the state, to find more than 50. For that, they had recourse to a means which displeases most people; they issued a forced loan which, according to the ordinary result of this kind of tax, caused many exactions and was not half covered. From 37 millions, the needs and expenses eventually rose to 60. The court of Cassel[1] had the pretension to rival the splendor of that of

---

[1] Kassel, capital of the kingdom of Westphalia from 1807 to 1813.

the Tuileries. The young sovereign so gave way to all his inclinations that I have heard it said . . . that, with the exception of three or four women respectable by their age, there was scarcely one at the palace over the fidelity of whom His Majesty had not acquired some rights. . . .

The luxury of the court, its disorders, and the uneasy state of the country caused the detestation of France and of the emperor, to whom all was attributed, and if this uneasiness did not produce an immediate outbreak, it was because the natural resignation of the Germans was increased by the terror caused by the close alliance of the King of Westphalia with the colossus of French power. . . . So, when in 1813, the Russian troops entered Westphalia, Jérôme's subjects regarded that moment as that of their deliverance.

55

NAPOLEON BONAPARTE

Letter to Joseph Bonaparte, King of Naples
July 30, 1806

When Napoleon encountered opposition, he did not hesitate to crush it by force. In this letter to Joseph, written soon after his brother had become king of Naples, Napoleon urges him to employ terror to bring a local rebellion to heel and set an example for his entire realm.

I am pleased you sent six infantry and two cavalry regiments to Cassano. That is enough to subdue all Calabria and trounce the English. . . .

You will have Naples and Sicily, you will be recognized by all Europe; but if you don't take more vigorous measures than you have so far, you will be shamefully dethroned upon the outbreak of continental war.

Above all, you are too good for your country. You must disarm, judge, and deport . . . The Kingdom of Italy produces for me 1,040,000

Correspondance de Napoléon, ed. Maximilien Vox (Paris: Gallimard, 1943), 339–42.

Milanese pounds; the kingdoms of Naples and Sicily must deliver as much; without this you will have nothing. You must have in your service 3,000 Corsicans, 6,000 Swiss, and no more than 6,000 Neapolitans. You do not employ enough Neapolitan officers who served in the Army of Italy. Follow my political principles; make the army patriotic, employ officers who are partisans of France and have shown energy; they will never betray you. . . .

The First Swiss Regiment is composed of men who served in France and who will be loyal. The Corsicans will be faithful to you, and you can recruit them easily. The Neapolitan patriots who were in France . . . will be loyal. I do not speak of the French army. . . . France will need all of her troops, and probably I will only be able to lend you two or three regiments.

Heed what I say: the destiny of your reign depends on your conduct upon retaking Calabria.

Do not pardon. Execute at least 600 rebels. They have cut the throats of even more of my soldiers. Burn the houses of the 30 principal leaders of the villages and give the army their property. Disarm all the inhabitants and pillage five or six of the worst-behaved villages. Order the soldiers to spare the loyal cities. Confiscate the communal properties of the rebel villages and give them to the army. Above all, disarm vigorously.

Since you compare the Neapolitans to the Corsicans, remember that when Niolo was taken, 40 rebels were hung from trees. The terror was so great, there was no more trouble.

Plaisance revolted; on my return from the Grand Army, I sent Junot,[2] who claimed the country had not risen up. . . . I ordered him to burn two villages and execute the leaders of the revolt, among whom were six priests. It was done and the country was subjugated. . . .

You see the terror the Queen[3] inspires; certainly, I do not propose that you imitate her; but it is still true that she is a power. If you act with vigor and energy, neither the Calabrese nor anyone else will budge for 30 years.

I finish my letter as I began it. You will be king of Naples; you will have three or four years of peace. If you are a do-nothing king, if you do not hold the reins with a firm and decided hand, if you listen to the opinion of a people which knows not what it wants, if you do not

----

[2] Andoche Junot (1771–1813), one of Napoleon's generals.

[3] Marie-Caroline, queen of Naples. Dethroned and replaced by Joseph, she led an armed struggle against the Napoleonic regime.

destroy ancient abuses and usurpations so as to enrich yourself, if you do not levy the taxes you need to keep in your service the French, Corsicans, Swiss, and Neapolitans, as well as equip warships, you will accomplish nothing at all; and in four years, instead of being useful to me, you will harm me by depriving me of resources.

Since Calabria revolted, why not take half of its properties and give them to the army. That would be a very useful resource to you and also set an example for the future.

Only extraordinary measures and vigor, not weakness, change and reform states.

56

LOUIS-FRANÇOIS LEJEUNE

Smuggling and the Continental System

1895

While all of continental Europe was within reach of his armies, Napoleon's mortal enemy, Great Britain, was protected by the English Channel. As long as Britain contested his dominance of the continent and continued to support opposition to him, Napoleon believed, the empire would remain insecure. With the French naval defeat at the Battle of Trafalgar (October 21, 1805), his last hope of invading Britain was dashed. Napoleon had no other way of attacking the island-nation than closing the ports of continental Europe to its trade. The economic and social impact of the continental blockade was enormous in Britain and Europe and throughout the Atlantic world. This extract from the memoir of General Louis-François Lejeune (1775–1848) describes the ruses employed by smugglers in Hamburg in 1810.

While taking the coach from Hamburg to Altona, I thought about many subjects; this country which lives exclusively on commerce, but

Louis-François Lejeune, *Mémoires du général Lejeune*, vol. 1 (Paris: Firmin Didot, 1895), 100–101.

whose ports are now closed; this Elbe river, once covered with vessels and a forest of masts, which is now devoid of shipping; this ingenious smuggling capable of overcoming the vigilance and rigors of the continental blockade, etc.

In thinking of all these misfortunes, I thought back on the previous night, at the gates of Hamburg. It had been very difficult to pass through a crowd of people who were looking at a curious spectacle. For some time, the guards had been saddened by the great mortality that seemed to reign in the city and daily sent surprising numbers of victims to the cemetery. Burials succeeded one another at a frightening pace. That day, one of the guards . . . had the idea of putting to his mouth the iron pick he had plunged into one of the many wheelbarrows of sand that the workers brought daily for construction in the city, and he found it was sweet. This made him realize that the wheelbarrow contained raw sugar, smuggled in and disguised under a bit of sand; the post was thereby alerted and, out of prudence, began to search even the hearses that were returning from funeral services: they found them full of sugar and percale. The crowd laughed and joked about this surprise, even while regretting that the trick, which had not cost a single life, had been discovered to the detriment of trade.

57

INHABITANTS OF PRESTON

Petition to the House of Commons

March 23, 1812

This petition from the inhabitants of the town of Preston in northwest England to the British House of Commons reveals how blockade-induced economic hardship put pressure on the British government for sweeping political reform.

The Parliamentary Debates from the Year 1803 to the Present Time, ed. T. C. Hansard, vol. 22 (London: 1812), 108–9.

The major part of the Petitioners are actually suffering, and all of them are compelled to see many thousands of their fellow-townsmen and neighbors suffer great hardships, for want of the common necessaries of life, which is not in the power, by all the exertions they can use, to procure for themselves and families, as the House will readily believe, when the Petitioners assure them . . . that the wages of a respectable body of artisans resident in that once flourishing town and the neighborhood are less by more than one half of what they were previously to the war with France, which began in 1793, whilst the price of every necessary article of subsistence has risen since that time in more than a twofold proportion; and that . . . these and like distresses, to which most of their beloved countrymen are at this time subjected, are attributable, as an immediate cause to the war in which the country is at present engaged; the Petitioners, therefore, are most anxious that if there exist any possibility of obtaining a peace, consistently with our honor and security, negotiations may be immediately entered into for the attainment of this desirable object; this anxiety, however, . . . is not created in them by any dread of the enemy; but being unacquainted with any desirable object, to the attainment of which a prosecution of the war will be conducive, they are desirous that no opportunity may be omitted of entering into negotiations for the restoration of the blessings of peace and amity; and that . . . the primary and principal causes of the evils they have enumerated, and of many others . . . are to be found in the admitting into the House of persons sent from old and decayed boroughs, who are, in most cases, returned at the instigation of ministers of the crown, or peers of the realm, contrary to the express tenor of our laws and constitution; and in the admittance also into the House of many minor placemen and pensioners, who have an interest different, and, in most cases, in opposition to the great body of the Commons of the United Kingdom, whom they ought to represent.

7

Napoleon and the Atlantic World

Colonial Ambitions

58

EUSTACHE BRUIX

Speech to the Legislature on the Reestablishment of Slavery

May 20, 1802

When Napoleon took power, France's overseas empire was a shadow of its former self. The revolutionary wars had resulted in the loss of French Caribbean sugar islands, Atlantic fisheries, African slaving bases, and Indian entrepôts to Britain. Above all, France's greatest colony, Saint-Domingue, had become effectively independent under the leadership of Pierre-Dominique Toussaint Louverture (1743–1803), a former slave who had led his people in a successful struggle to overthrow slavery. The First Consul came under enormous pressure to restore France's colonial empire. For creoles, merchants, and naval leaders alike, this meant reimposing slavery, seen as the key to colonial prosperity. The following document is an excerpt from a speech delivered to the Tribunate by Admiral and Tribune Eustache Bruix (1759–1805) calling for the reestablishment of slavery.

Archives Parlementaires, series II, vol. 3, 752–53.

Doubtless it is unfortunate that part of the human race is condemned by nature or social institutions to servile labor and slavery. But we will heed the lessons of our experience and those provided by the example of our rivals. . . .

In effect, our islands' commercial monopoly, the exclusive right to bring them raw materials and manufactured goods and return with their productions, can alone ensure us the double gain of exportation enjoyed by other European nations. . . . The taste for our arts, habits, and luxuries bind the Creole to us. The free black, less active, without desires, would disdain our continent's productions. He prefers manioc to grain, sugar liquor to wine. The tropical climate makes him reject clothing and thus exempts him from using the products of our industry. . . .

Could France rely on colonies peopled primarily by free blacks? Their interests would soon diverge from the home country's, because the Antillean negro's absent homeland is Africa. The sacrifices joyfully made by the colonist, attached to France by common culture, relations of friendship, ties of blood, . . . would seem heavy to the African. Soon, he would elude the exclusive commercial regime without which our neighbors would take the profit of our colonial administration. . . . If blacks acquire land, their harvest will pass into contraband commerce. Thus, property and power must be in the hands of a few whites, and negroes, in great numbers, must be slaves. . . .

Without our slave colonies, no more trade with Africa, no more way of increasing our fisheries. . . . In Europe, our agriculture and industry would decline, along with our East Indian commerce; our naval power would suffer gravely from reductions in sailors and workers. All this would result from freedom for the blacks.

59

NAPOLEON BONAPARTE

Letter to Toussaint Louverture

1802

Along with the thorny question of slavery, the problem of restoring French authority over Saint-Domingue haunted Napoleon's colonial policy. These two imperatives did not mesh easily. Attempting to reimpose slavery in Saint-Domingue would reignite the vicious war that had devastated the island during the past ten years. But without slavery, believed many in the colonial lobby, Saint-Domingue would hardly be worth recovering. Napoleon proceeded cautiously, avoiding any hint that slavery might be reestablished while flattering Toussaint and reminding him of his duty to France. In the following letter, Napoleon urges Toussaint to cooperate with General Victoire-Emmanuel Leclerc (1772– 1802), Napoleon's brother-in-law, who had just been named Captain-General of Saint-Domingue and was about to lead an expeditionary force to the island.

Peace with England and the powers of Europe . . . enables the government to attend to Saint-Domingue. We send Citizen Leclerc, our brother-in-law, as Captain-General, to be the colony's chief magistrate. He is accompanied by forces necessary to make the sovereignty of the French people respected. Under these circumstances, we are disposed to hope that you will prove to us and France the sincerity of the sentiments you have constantly expressed. . . . We respect you and wish to recognize and proclaim your great services to the French people. We owe it to you and your brave blacks that their colors still fly over Saint-Domingue. Summoned by your talents and circumstance to supreme command, you ended civil war, halted persecution, and restored honor, religion, and the worship of God, source of all things.

Marcus Rainsford, *An Historical Account of the Black Empire of Hayti: Comprehending a View of the Principal Transactions in the Revolution of Saint Domingo with Its Antient and Modern State* (London: James Cundee, 1805), 273–76.

Surrounded by enemies and without the mother country able to succor or sustain you, your situation has rendered legitimate your constitution. . . . But now that circumstances are so happily changed, you will be the first to render homage to the sovereignty of the nation, which reckons you one of its most illustrious citizens. . . . Contrary conduct would contradict our impression of you. It would deprive you of your claims to the gratitude and good offices of the Republic, and would dig under your feet a precipice which, while it consumed you, would increase the misery of those brave blacks, whose courage we love, and whom we would regret punishing for rebellion.

Assist the Captain-General with your counsel, influence, and talents. What can you desire?—freedom of the blacks? You know that everywhere we have gone, we have given it to people who lacked it. Do you desire consideration, honor, fortune? With the services you have rendered and can still render, and with our esteem for you, you should not doubt that consideration, fortune, and honors await you.

Inform the people of Saint-Domingue that French concern for their happiness has often been thwarted by the imperious circumstances of war; that the men who came from the Continent to sow division were products of the factionalism that destroyed the country; that in the future, peace and governmental power ensure their prosperity and freedom. Tell them that if liberty is their greatest desire, they can only enjoy it as French citizens, and that every act contrary to the interests of the country . . . would be a crime against national sovereignty which would eclipse their services and make Saint-Domingue the theater of a cruel war in which fathers and children would massacre each other.

And you, General, remember that while you are the first of your color to have attained such great power and distinguished himself by bravery and military talents, you are also responsible for their conduct before God and our self.

60

NAPOLEON BONAPARTE

Confidential Instructions to General Leclerc

1801

Napoleon's true intentions regarding slavery in Saint-Domingue are difficult to ascertain, although his determination to return the island to French rule was crystal clear. The following excerpt from Napoleon's secret instructions to General Leclerc exemplifies this mixture of ambiguity and decisiveness and leaves ample room for interpretation.

The French nation will never enslave men it has recognized as free. Thus, all the blacks of Saint-Domingue will live like those in Guadeloupe today.

Your conduct will follow three phases.

In the first, you will disarm only those blacks who are in rebellion.

In the third, you will disarm them all.

In the first phase, you will not be very demanding: you will negotiate with Toussaint and promise him all he desires in order to take possession of the strategic points and establish yourself in the country.

Once this first goal has been achieved, you will become stricter. You will order him to respond categorically to the proclamation and my letter. You will order him to come to Le Cap.

In the interviews you may have with Moyse, Dessalines, and Toussaint's other generals, you will treat them well.

Win over Christophe, Clairveaux, Maurepas, Félix, Romain, Jasmain, etc., and all other blacks favorable to the whites. In the first phase, confirm their ranks and positions. In the third phase, send them all to France with their ranks if they served well during the second phase.

In the first phase, all Toussaint's principal agents, both whites and

---

Lettres du Général Leclerc, commandant en chef de l'armée de Saint-Domingue en 1802, ed. Paul Roussier (Paris: Ernest Leroux, 1937), 269–72.

men of color, ought to be honored and confirmed in their grades. In the final phase, they should be sent to France with their grades if they behaved well in the second, but otherwise as deportees.

During the first phase, all blacks in positions of responsibility should be flattered and treated well, but, in general, you should try to undermine their popularity and power. Toussaint, Moyse, and Dessalines ought to be well treated during the first phase, but sent to France in the final phase, either under arrest or with their rank, depending on their conduct during the second phase.

The first phase should not last more than 15 days. If it does, you have been tricked.

Consider Toussaint subdued only if he has come to Le Cap or Port-au-Prince and sworn a loyalty oath to the Republic before the French army. On that day, you must quietly, and with honor and consideration, put him on a frigate and send him to France. If you can, arrest Moyse and Dessalines at the same time, or pursue them mercilessly, and send to France all white partisans of Toussaint and all blacks in positions of responsibility whom you suspect of ill-will. Declare Moyse and Dessalines traitors to the homeland and enemies of the French people. Set the troops in motion and do not rest until you have their heads and have dispersed and disarmed their supporters.

If after the first 15 or 20 days, it is impossible to bring back Toussaint, you must publish a proclamation declaring that if, after a certain delay, he has not come to swear an oath of loyalty to the Republic, he will be declared a traitor and, when the delay expires, you will begin a merciless war.

Even if a few thousand blacks are still wandering in the hills and hiding in the countryside, [you] should nonetheless consider the second phase over and promptly begin the third. This will be the moment for assuring permanent French possession of the colony. And the same day, throughout the entire colony, you should arrest all untrustworthy men in positions of responsibility, whatever their color, and embark the black generals, whatever their mores, patriotism, and services, while nonetheless maintaining their ranks and promising that they will be well treated in France.

All whites who have served under Toussaint and bloodied their hands in the massacres of Saint-Domingue will be sent directly to Guyana.

All blacks who have behaved well, but whose ranks prevent them from remaining on the island will be sent to Brest.

All blacks and men of color who have behaved badly, whatever their ranks, will be sent to the Mediterranean and landed in a Corsican port.

If Toussaint, Dessalines, or Moyse have been captured under arms, they will be judged by a military commission within 24 hours and shot as rebels.

Whatever happens, in the course of the third phase you should disarm all negroes, regardless of the party to which they belong, and return them to field work. . . .

White women who prostituted themselves to negroes, whatever their rank, will be sent to Europe.

Colonial Retreat

61

GENERAL LECLERC

Letter to Napoleon Bonaparte

October 7, 1802

Leclerc's expedition soon ran into trouble. When word arrived in the island that the French were reimposing slavery in Guadeloupe, Haitians rose in mass against the French. Fighting raged across the island. Despite having won some early victories and having captured Toussaint Louverture, who was sent to France in chains, the French army was rapidly worn down by combat and disease. Leclerc himself succumbed to yellow fever in November 1802. The remnants of his army surrendered a year later. This letter to Napoleon from Leclerc, written less than a month before his death, paints a grim picture.

Lettres du Général Leclerc, commandant en chef de l'armée de Saint-Domingue en 1802, ed. Paul Roussier (Paris: Ernest Leroux, 1937), 253–59.

[Initially] I held the country without any real forces. Then at the end of Thermidor, the war began and doubled my losses. At the end of Fructidor my army and reinforcements had been destroyed. On seeing my weakness, the blacks grew audacious. . . .

You will perhaps blame me for not having eliminated the black leaders earlier, but remember that I was never in a position to do so, and that I was planning on acting against them this season. . . . If, from very good, my position has become very bad, the reason is the disease that destroyed my army, the premature reestablishment of slavery in Guadeloupe, and the newspapers and letters from France that talk only of slavery. . . .

We must destroy all the negroes of the mountains, men and women, and keep only children under twelve, destroy half of those of the plain, and allow not a single man of color [with officer rank] to remain in the colony. Otherwise it will never be calm, . . . and civil war will compromise our possession of the country. If you wish to be master of Saint-Domingue, you must send me 12,000 men without wasting a single day. . . .

If you cannot send me [these] troops, . . . Saint-Domingue will be forever lost to France.

Personal note from Leclerc to Bonaparte, attached to the above letter:

Since I have been here, I have seen only the spectacle of fires, insurrections, murders, of the dead and dying. My soul is withered, and no joyful thought can ever make me forget these hideous scenes. I fight here against blacks, whites, misery, lack of money, and my discouraged army. . . .

62

FRANÇOIS BARBÉ-MARBOIS

The Sale of Louisiana

1829

With the definitive loss of Saint-Domingue and the resumption of hostilities with Great Britain, Napoleon abandoned his colonial projects. Possession of Louisiana, recovered from Spain by secret treaty in October 1801, no longer served any purpose. Even worse, word that France had regained the colony was beginning to arouse American feelings against France. Seeing Louisiana as a liability, Napoleon resolved to sell it to the Americans. In the following document, minister of the treasury and former colonial administrator François Barbé-Marbois (1745–1837) recounts discussing Louisiana with Napoleon.

Napoleon: "I know the full value of Louisiana, and I have been desirous of repairing the fault of the French negotiator who abandoned it in 1763. A few lines of a treaty have restored it to me, and I have scarcely recovered it when I expect to lose it. But if it escapes from me, it shall one day cost dearer to those who oblige me to strip myself of it than to those to whom I wish to deliver it. The English have successively taken from France, Canada, Cape Breton, Newfoundland, Nova Scotia, and the richest portions of Asia. They are engaged in exciting troubles in Saint-Domingue. They shall not have the Mississippi which they covet. Louisiana is nothing in comparison with their conquests in all parts of the globe, and yet the jealousy they feel at the restoration of this colony to the sovereignty of France, acquaints me with their wish to take possession of it, and it is thus that they will begin the war. They have twenty ships of war in the Gulf of Mexico, they sail over those seas as sovereigns, whilst our affairs in Saint-Domingue have been growing worse every day since the death of Leclerc. The conquest of Louisiana would be easy, if they only took the trouble to

François Barbé-Marbois, *The History of Louisiana: Particularly of the Cession of That Colony to the United States of America* (Baton Rouge: Louisiana State University Press, 1977), 263–66, 274–75, 312.

effect a landing there. I have not a moment to lose in putting it out of their reach. . . . I think of ceding it to the United States. . . . They only ask of me one town in Louisiana, but I already consider the colony as entirely lost, and it appears to me that in the hands of this growing power, it will be more useful to the policy and even to the commerce of France, than if I should attempt to keep it."

Barbé-Marbois: "We should not hesitate to make a sacrifice of that which is about to slip away from us. War with England is inevitable; shall we be able with very inferior naval forces to defend Louisiana against that power? . . . The country is scarcely at all inhabited; you have not fifty soldiers there. Where are your means of sending garrisons? Can we restore fortifications that are in ruins, and construct a long chain of forts upon a frontier of 1,200 miles? If England lets you undertake these things, it is because they will drain your resources, and she will feel a secret joy in seeing you exhaust yourself in efforts of which she alone will derive the profit. You will send out a squadron; but, while it is crossing the ocean, the colony will fall, and the squadron will in its turn be in danger. Louisiana is open to the English from the north by the great lakes, and if, to the south, they show themselves at the mouth of the Mississippi, New Orleans will immediately fall into their hands. What consequence is it to the inhabitants to whom they are subject, if their country is not to cease to be a colony? This conquest would be still easier to the Americans; they can reach the Mississippi by several navigable rivers, and to be masters of the country it will be sufficient from them to enter it. The population and resources of one of these two neighbors every day increase; and the other has maritime means sufficient to take possession of everything that can advance her commerce. The colony has existed for a century, and in spite of efforts and sacrifices of every kind, the last accounts of its population and resources attest to its weakness. If it becomes a French colony and acquires increased importance, there will be in its very prosperity a germ of independence, which will not be long in developing itself. The more it flourishes, the less chances we have of preserving it. Nothing is more uncertain than the future fate of the European colonies in America. The exclusive right which the parent states exercise over these remote settlements becomes every day more and more precarious. The people feel humbled at being dependent on a small country in Europe, and will liberate themselves, as soon as they have a consciousness of their own strength. . . ."

Napoleon: "Irresolution and deliberation are no longer in season. I renounce Louisiana. . . . I know the price of what I abandon, and I have sufficiently proved the importance that I attach to this province, since my first diplomatic act with Spain had aimed at recovering it. I renounce it with the greatest regret. To attempt obstinately to retain it would be folly. I direct you to negotiate this affair with the envoys of the United States. . . . Perhaps it will be objected to me, that the Americans may be found too powerful for Europe in two or three centuries: but my foresight does not embrace such remote fears. Besides, we may hereafter expect rivalries among the members of the Union. The confederations, that are called perpetual, only last till one of the contracting parties finds it to its interest to break them, and it is to prevent the danger, to which the colossal power of England exposes us, that I would provide a remedy. . . . This accession of territory strengthens forever the power of the United States; and I have just given to England a maritime rival, that will sooner or later humble her pride."

Napoleon and Latin America

63

JOSEPH BONAPARTE

Instructions to Secret Agents in Spanish America
1810

After the collapse of his dream of an American empire, Napoleon focused almost exclusively on Europe, where victories over Austria, Russia, and Prussia allowed him to assemble a collection of satellite kingdoms for his siblings to rule. But with his invasion of Spain in 1807 and the installation of his brother Joseph as its king, Napoleon once again turned his attention to the Americas. By severing the colonies' links with Spain and overthrowing its king, the invasion had generated great confusion in Spanish America. Napoleon hoped to exploit this situation by sending to the Spanish colonies emissaries who would provoke pro-Napoleonic ris-

Documentos de Cancillerias Europeas sobre la Independencia Venezolana, ed. Caracciolo Parra-Perez, vol. 1 (Caracas: Biblioteca de la Academia Nacional de la Historia, 1962), 69–71.

ings against local, royalist authorities. The following document is an excerpt from Joseph Bonaparte's instructions to his Baltimore-based spymaster in the United States.

The sole goal of these agents is to persuade the creoles that His Imperial and Royal Majesty wants only to liberate Spanish America, for so long sunk in slavery, win the friendship of the inhabitants, and secure free trade for the two Americas. To gain independence for Spanish America, promise all necessary reinforcements.... Each commissar or chief agent will study the nature of the district in which he is undertaking his mission and the character of its inhabitants: this will easily identify the best people to receive the necessary instructions to win over the populace and explain the advantages of independence. He will announce that the huge sums to be spent in Europe will then circulate in the provinces of America, increasing their resources, commerce, and prosperity; that their ports will be open to all nations. Emphasize the advantages of freedom of agriculture and of all the objects currently prohibited by the Spanish government, like saffron, wine, olives, flax, thread; the benefits that will come from the establishment of all kinds of industry, from the abolition of the tobacco, gunpowder, and playing-card monopolies. To attain this object more easily (since most of these people are not civilized), the agents will make themselves agreeable to the governors, intendants, priests, and prelates. They will not spare money or any other means of winning them over, especially the ecclesiastics. They will subtly get them to persuade their penitents, when they go to confession, that it is the best moment to seek independence; ... that Napoleon has been sent by God to castigate the pride and tyranny of kings, and that it would be a mortal sin to resist his will. The agents will seize every opportunity to remind them of the oppression they suffer at the hands of the Europeans, and the disdain with which they are treated. They will also remind the Indians of the cruelties of the first conquistadors, the horrible treatment they inflicted upon their legitimate king. They will detail the injustice inflicted upon them daily by the unworthy bureaucrats appointed by the viceroys and governors, at the expense of those who deserved these employments and rewards. They will direct the attention of the people toward the superior talents of certain creoles, of meritorious individuals of the lower class who have been left in obscurity, and will underline the contrast between them and the European officials and churchmen. They will highlight the difference between the United States and Spanish America, the comfort the Americans enjoy, their progress in commerce, agriculture, and navigation, the pleasure to be free from European domination and enjoy self-determination. They will assure them that, once separated from Spain, America will lay down the law to Europe. All the agents, both superior and subaltern, should note who declares themselves as friends of liberty. The subaltern agents will transmit their lists to their superiors who will report to my envoys in the United States. They will inform me so I can reward each individual. My agents will not speak against the Inquisition or Church, and in their conversations will insist on the necessity of this holy tribunal and the usefulness of the clergy. The insurrectional flag will feature these words: "Long Live the Catholic, Apostolic, and Roman Religion! Down with Bad Government!" In addition, they will point out to the Indians how much happier they would be if they ruled their own countries, if they were free from the tyrannical tribute they pay to a foreign monarch. Finally, they will tell the people that their supposed monarch is in the power of the restorer of liberty, of the universal legislator, in a word, Napoleon. By all possible means, these agents must demonstrate to the people the advantages of a new government.

64

VICEROY OF NEW SPAIN

Denunciation of Bonapartist Subversion

1810

The royalist colonial authorities took the threat of Napoleonic subversion seriously, for they were painfully aware of the depth and diversity of social discontent in Spanish America. The following document, an excerpt from an 1810 proclamation of the Viceroy of New Spain, Archbishop Francisco Javier de Lizana y Beaumont (1749–1815), gives a sense of the royalists' insecurity.

Coleccion de Documentos para la Historia de la Guerra de Independencia de Mexico de 1808 a 1821, ed. J. E. Hernandez y Davalos, vol. 2 (Mexico, 1878; Nendeln, Liechtenstein: Kraus reprint, 1968), 11–15.

Vassals of Ferdinand VII, everyone under my paternal care and government, there are two things that bring misfortune to the people, fear and disunion. Fear makes them cowards and slaves; disunion weakens them and invites oppression. Be courageous and valiant. Be ever united in brotherhood. Because I desire your well-being, I pray for you like the great apostle Paul to the sons of Corinth, in the name of our lord Jesus Christ, that you all share the same ideas and feelings. It pains me that suddenly there are divisions and diverse opinions among you. Today, we should all be of one heart like the first Christians, since we all profess the same religion and grieve for a suffering king. They want to steal our goods, enslave us, and, worse, divert us from the path of salvation. . . . Like a good disciple of Lucifer, [Bonaparte] knows that, even in heaven, division was the ruin of the angels. . . .

Napoleon will not destroy Ferdinand's empire in Mexico. . . . The proximity of Spain to France, their trade and friendship, and those ungrateful serpents who fed on that incautious mother's breast gave Napoleon the practical knowledge he used to conquer our home country. But console yourselves. Bonaparte underestimates New Spain's capacity to resist. He knows not your character and enlightenment. He considers the inhabitants of this kingdom incapable of sustaining a campaign and believes there are neither soldiers, discipline, cannon, nor leaders here to resist the feeble attempts of his troops to dominate us. He thinks some of you are sunk in effeminate opulence while the rest suffer under an unbearable yoke, buried in the mines where he is determined to lock you all up. Idiot! You would be confounded if you saw the number, agility, and skill of our soldiers, the bravery and courage of our officers, the expertise and gallantry of our military leaders. You would be astonished to feel our hatred for your diabolical person and the French name, our love for Ferdinand, the patriotism that animates us, and our consuming desire to avenge the outrages committed upon the common fatherland, and to extinguish the race and memory of the Napoleonic monsters of irreligion and despotism.

Vassals of Ferdinand VII, we have courage to spare, we have people and resources the tyrant cannot imagine. Besides, we know his purposes; to enslave this free and happy people, the envy of the world; to seize the land of gold and silver; . . . to plunder our temples, sack our houses, rape our virgins and matrons, giving his soldiers two hours of pillaging and raping in each town. . . . This is the recompense and wage with which the monster pays his troops.

And will you allow this, generous descendants of those heroes who shed their blood in the Old World to free Spain from Saracen domination, to defend the Catholic religion, and establish the house of Charles V? . . . Ah! I am bathed in delight when I see your exalted patriotism and loyalty, your burning courage banishing fear from your hearts. . . .

But it is not enough to banish fear, it is essential to be united in brotherhood. Vassals of Ferdinand VII, the tyrant Napoleon's only recourse is to sow disunion among brothers. Neither his military expertise nor the number and courage of his troops have made him the master of foreign kingdoms. His Machiavellian policy is the secret of his intrigues—he has artfully sown and fermented discord, taking advantage of it to weaken nations and peoples, and subjugate them.

Among his vile satellites are many people who have valuable practical knowledge of America, and who have made him conceive that the distinction between Creoles and Peninsulars[1] is a source of rivalry, envy, resentment, and even hatred and diversity of opinions about the public cause. . . .

For 300 years, the simple names of Creoles and Peninsulars have served only to indicate the birthplace of Spaniards inhabiting this New World; but never have they been used as a bar of distinction for esteem, occupations, honors, nor a distinction in the eyes of the law or the monarch. A Peninsular is a European-born Spaniard; a Creole is a Spaniard born in America. The Peninsular is the Creole's father; the Creole is the Peninsular's son; the Peninsular is the husband of the Creole's daughter; the Creole is the grandfather of the Peninsular's sons. What else? Creoles and Peninsulars are like two brothers, or like uncle and nephew; because all of them are sons of Spaniards. . . . Who but the thoughtless conqueror of the world could imagine bitter competition and discord between father and son, husband and wife? . . .

The happy Creole gives his daughter and wealth to the European Spaniard; he affectionately loves her and takes care of the wealth, preserving, increasing, and bequeathing it to the American Spaniard's grandsons. The European Spaniard, noble and grateful, thanks heaven every day for his wife and American sons; he blesses the bread he eats, the ground he walks on, the gold he spends, the pure, healthy, and warm air he peacefully enjoys 2,000 leagues from Bonaparte's poisonous shadow; and the American-born Spaniard, a generous gentleman, protects the European, entrusts him his Hacienda, and

---

[1] *Peninsulars*: In the original Spanish, the word is "gauchipines."

welcomes him into his family. Could Napoleon believe that among these people, intimately attached by love, virtue, blood, and interest, there would ever be mortal quarrels, implacable hatred, natural aversion that would have any influence on the sacred interests of religion, king, or fatherland?

65

RICHARD RUSH

Letter to James Monroe

April 1817

The extent to which Napoleonic subversion contributed to the Latin American independence movement is unclear. What is certain is that Latin American independence signaled the end of the old Atlantic order that had prevailed since 1492. This transformation produced dramatic strategic realignments. The following document, a letter written in several installments in April 1817 from acting U.S. secretary of state Richard Rush (1780–1859) to President James Monroe (1758–1831), illustrates the nature of this geopolitical revolution.

The French minister [Hyde de Neuville] called on me and spoke of the struggle between Spain and her colonies. Bonaparte, he said, as was well known, when he found that he was not likely to subdue Spain, next became anxious to sever the colonies from her. During the later part of his reign, he had sent emissaries to the colonies to cooperate towards his ends.

He expressed a strong wish to know what were the real sentiments and intentions . . . of our government in regard to this struggle. . . . He would not scruple to add in confidence to me that France looked upon this struggle with the same eyes that he presumed we did, vis, that if the colonies were destined to become independent, we did not wish England to reap the benefit of it.

Monroe Papers (Washington: Library of Congress, 1960), microfilm reel 6.

April 25. The French minister called upon me again at the Department of State and renewed the topic of yesterday. I informed him that the President would be glad to hear through me whatever he might have to communicate relative to South America and Spain. That he might rely upon the cordial feeling of this government towards France, and its desire to cultivate upon just principles the most friendly intercourse with her. . . .

He now declared that France had no intention or wish to assist the colonies; on the contrary, perhaps her wishes were the other way. But that, as he believed, their independence was likely to be the result of the struggle if it went on, France wished England to be cut off from deriving the chief benefit of it, and was the more anxious on this point as he also believed that England was favoring their independence. In this condition of things, Spain, he said, continued to be full of anxiety to reclaim the colonies for herself. He believed that she could do so by changing her conduct towards them; by offering terms so conciliatory and just that a settlement of all past disputes and heart burnings would follow. . . .

He now approached his main object. He said that if the U.S. and France would . . . move in concert with Spain in this projected course of policy towards her colonies, advantageous commercial results might be secured to the three nations from which England could be excluded. France, he said, was disposed to act in this policy. . . .

April 30. Saw the French minister again. We talked largely about the colonies, his plan for a triple alliance having met no favor from the President. I gave into the idea that if other powers did not step forward, England would be likely to run away with the chief profit of their independence. The minister said that he was sure of it.

I then remarked that, if as he also seemed to believe, independence would come about, would it not be better that the U.S. should be the first to acknowledge it? Ought not other powers, as France, for example, to wish this, as England might thereby be prevented taking the lead? He made no reply. Surely, I said, as between England and the U.S., the powers of Europe, and France especially, would prefer that the U.S. should have the best standing with Spanish America. He admitted it.

8
Decline and Fall

The Spanish Ulcer

66

SUPREME GOVERNMENTAL JUNTA

Appeal to the Clergy
1808

The final years of Napoleon's empire offer an example of imperial over-reach. Ambition and pride drew Napoleon into a succession of military adventures that stretched his armies thin, bled them white, and under-mined their morale. Moreover, the same forces of nationalism that had inspired the French in their days of victory were now turned against them. The slide toward defeat was gradual, almost imperceptible. Napo-leon's invasion of Spain in 1807–1808 was the beginning of the end. After a six-year guerrilla war supported by regular troops from Britain, Portu-gal, and Spain, the French were finally driven out of the country. Tying down hundreds of thousands of soldiers, the struggle steadily drained French resources. The following document, an appeal from the Supreme Governmental Junta (the body formed to govern Spain in the place of the absent monarch, Ferdinand VII, and in opposition to the French-installed regime) to the Spanish bishops, indicates the importance of reli-gion in the uprising.

M. Chaulanges, A. G. Manry, and R. Sève, *Textes historiques, 1799–1815: L'époque de Napoléon* (Paris: Delagrave, 1960), 145–47.

The cause of our revolution was patriotism and love of religion, which happily still exists in this Catholic Kingdom; but these powerful motivations have lost their force and might disappear completely if we do not adopt decisive measures to revive and reinforce them. The Junta, which cannot tolerate for a moment the idea of losing both Fatherland and Religion, seeks the aid of ecclesiastics in this heroic task, for, if they have a direct interest in maintaining our holy religion, their mission is also best suited to inflaming the people which listens to them like oracles. . . .

The Fatherland's peril is obvious. . . . If Spain succumbs, can religion survive rule by an atheist who, when he tried to fool us with pompous promises, allowed his soldiers to profane churches, rape sacred virgins, and sacrifice the ministers of the altar? Who had his devilish agents write scandalous insults and indecent satires against the most sacred religious mysteries? Who outrageously dethroned the Sovereign Pontiff, visible head of the Church?[1] And if religion is lost, can we retain the moral virtues which, even in periods of corruption, have always preserved our country from the century's depravity? The Supreme Junta . . . is persuaded that Your Excellency, driven by the same sentiments, will be convinced of the necessity of reviving the faith of the believers and showing them that the current war is a holy and religious one: perhaps it would be appropriate to grant, as during the Crusades, indulgences to those who take up arms and send to the armies monks known for their virtue and eloquence to harangue the soldiers before battle. . . .

The French broke treaties and violated the laws of hospitality, a virtue that even savages respect; they hypocritically kidnapped our beloved King and the whole royal family; they destroyed our laws, rights, and customs; they sacked villages and cities, burnt houses, devastated the countryside, raped women, and, with unspeakable cruelty, sacrificed small children to their anger; in all the countries they have entered, they have taken young men from the paternal bosom to serve the tyrant's ambition; finally, they reduced entire nations to indigence. . . . If presented well and often, these facts . . . should convince [Spaniards] that the only alternative is victory or death. . . . It would be most appropriate to urge all parish priests, in private talks, sermons, and public acts, to paint for the people a true picture of its terrible fate if it does not defend itself vigorously. . . .

[1]A reference to the imprisonment of Pope Pius VII by Napoleon.

67

Civil Catechism, and Brief Compendium of the Obligations of the Spaniard

1808

The much-reprinted Civil Catechism, *selections from which appear below, uses a familiar form and stresses monarchical and religious themes to mobilize the Spanish people against the French occupiers. Yet the concluding section suggests that it would be a mistake to see it as an expression of hidebound conservatism.*

Who is the enemy of our happiness?
—The French emperor.

Who is this man?
—A new lord, infinitely bad, ambitious, source of all evil and end of all good; he combines all vices and evil deeds.

How many are his natures?
—Two, one diabolical, the other human. . . .

Where does Napoleon come from?
—From hell and sin. . . .

What are his attributes?
—Arrogance, evildoing, and despotism. . . .

Who are the French?
—Ex-Christians, and new heretics.

What led them to this unfortunate state?
—False philosophy and the liberty of their perverse customs.

Catecismo civil, y breve compendio de las obligaciones del español, conocimiento pratico de su libertad, y explicacion de su enemigo, my util en las actuales circunstancias, puesto en forma de dialogo (1808).

How do they serve their leader?
—Some by flattery, others by aiding his iniquity, and the rest by exterminating humanity.

Will his evil reign ever end?
—The wisest politicians feel that its ruin is very near.

What can save us from such an invader?
—Union, constancy, and arms.

Is it a sin to kill the French?
—Yes sir, but not those serving under Napoleon's banner.

Why isn't it a mortal sin to kill them?
—Since they are thieves, murderers, arsonists, and blasphemers, natural law requires that we kill them to free our brothers from so many evils.

What ideas should we take into battle?
—Salvation of the fatherland and defense of the state, our brothers, and the immortal glory of the nation.

Who must take up arms?
—All those chosen by the government as the most apt, well-disposed, and least useful to the population.

What must the rest do?
—Contribute generously with all the goods they have received from the fatherland and show patriotism.

Those who have nothing, what should they do?
—Pray to God for the success of Spanish arms, and occupy themselves with trade, crafts, or business. . . .

How has the tyrant occupied our towns?
—By deceit, treason, baseness, and perfidy.

And these means sufficed for them to usurp another's crown?
—No sir, on the contrary, they don't deserve our condescension, and we must resist with all our might a usurper king who uses such unjust and abominable methods.

What kind of happiness should we seek?
—That which they cannot give us.

What is it?
—Security of our rights and persons, free exercise of our sacred religion, and a government based on the actual customs of Spain and its relations with Europe.

But didn't we already have this?
—Yes sir, but it was disorganized by the despotism and indolence of the supreme authorities who governed us.

Who should remedy it?
—Spain, which alone has this right to the absolute exclusion of all foreigners.

Who will authorize this plan?
—Ferdinand VII, whom God wants to restore to the bosom of our eternal love.

68

CHARLES-FRANÇOIS FRANÇOIS

Atrocities of War

undated (nineteenth century)

Both sides of the Spanish War engaged systematically in horrific acts of brutality. This description of atrocities, echoed in other accounts as well as in the paintings of Goya, is from the diary of Captain Charles-François François (1774/5–1853).

L'épopée impériale racontée par la Grande Armée, ed. Théo Fleischman (Paris: Perrin, 1964), 163–64.

I saw officers, soldiers, even women slit open from uterus to stomach, with breasts cut off, men sawn in half, others whose penises had been cut off and placed in their mouths; others buried alive up to their shoulders with their genitals in their mouth, and others hung by their feet inside of chimneys, their heads consumed by fire; finally, at Val-de-Penas, I saw 53 men buried up to their shoulders around a house being used as a hospital where 400 men had had their throats slit, been cut into pieces, and cast into the streets and yards. Brave General René, . . . who had just joined General Dupont's army with his wife and child, was captured in the gorges of the Sierra Morena [and] . . . cut in half in front of his wife, after having watched her being raped; then the child was cut in half before its mother, who was finally murdered in the same manner. . . .

We found the bodies of our soldiers, whose noses, ears, limbs, and tongues had been cut off, and others whose fingernails and eyes had been torn out.

In the town of Manzannares, most of the inhabitants fled to escape our vengeance, as they had assassinated 1,200 sick soldiers lodged there. Here is how the massacre was described to me. The inhabitants of the town went to the hospital where there were about 1,200 sick soldiers, whose throats they cut and whom they cut into pieces (I saw them myself). A Spaniard of the town told me that an officer who was there was led by the crowd to the main square where, after having had his eyelids and fingernails removed, he was cut into pieces and fed to the pigs; that the healthier soldiers were stoned, cut into pieces, and strewn in the road; that only one escaped and was saved by an inhabitant, but had already had his ears cut off. I saw this poor man, who had been driven mad. . . . Some Spaniards said these crimes were inspired by the priests' advice to the inhabitants.

To Russia and Back

69

DENIS DAVYDOV

Partisan Warfare

1820–1822

On the night of June 24–25, 1812, Napoleon invaded Russia with a multinational army of more than 600,000 soldiers drawn from all parts of his empire. Five months later, he led out fewer than 100,000 survivors. The root cause of the war was Russian fear of the empire's growing power. At the end of 1810, Czar Alexander withdrew from the continental blockade. Napoleon resolved to retaliate and deployed against the outnumbered Russians the largest army Europe had ever seen. The Russian army retreated before the invaders and, despite fighting several bloody battles, managed to extricate itself. Meanwhile, Napoleon's armies were diminished daily by casualties and the need to detach large numbers of troops to guard increasingly lengthy supply lines. One aristocratic Russian officer, Denis Davydov (1784–1839), perceived this vulnerability and sought to exploit it by organizing partisan warfare against the French rear. Below is an excerpt from Davydov's memoirs.

The enemy army was streaming toward the capital. Innumerable carts, transports, convoys, and marauding bands followed behind them on both sides of the road for a distance of 30–40 miles.

This multitude, subject to no form of discipline, committed all manner of violent excesses. A broad band of territory had been laid waste, consumed by fire, and whole communities were fleeing from the onslaught with their remaining possessions, headed nobody knew where. As for my party, it is important to stress that our progress was becoming increasingly dangerous as we put more distance between us

Denis Davydov, *In the Service of the Tsar against Napoleon: The Memoirs of Denis Davydov, 1806–1814*, ed. and trans. Gregory Troubetzkoy (London: Greenhill, 1999), 84–89.

and the army. Even places left untouched by the enemy posed many difficulties for us.

Local volunteer militia groups habitually barred the way. In every village the gates were closed; young and old manned them with pitchforks, pikes, hatchets and sometimes firearms. As we approached each settlement, one of us had to ride up and parley with the inhabitants, telling them that we were Russians, that we were coming to help them and to protect the orthodox churches. Often the reply came in the form of a shot or an axe thrown at us. Providence saved us from these missiles!

We could have skirted the villages, but I wanted to spread the word that troops were returning, strengthen the determination of the peasants to defend themselves and persuade them to inform us of approaching enemy troops. . . .

I often asked these villagers: "Why did you suppose we were French?" They invariably answered: "Well, you see, my dear sir," pointing to my uniform, "they tell us this resembles their outfits." . . .

Only then did I learn by experience that in a people's war one must not only speak the local language, but also adopt their ways and their clothes. I put on a peasant smock, let my beard grow, and instead of the Order of St. Anne, I hung an icon of St. Nicholas around my neck and began talking to the people in their own dialect. . . .

[I instructed the villagers] how to deal with the bands of marauders who, for the time being, outnumbered them.

"Receive them in a friendly way," I told them. "Do plenty of bowing (because not knowing Russian, bows will be better understood) and bring out all you have in the way of food, and especially drink. Put them to bed drunk and when you see that they are properly asleep, grab all their weapons . . . and do what God has ordained against enemies of Christ's church and your motherland."

"Once you have wiped them out, bury their bodies in the animal barn or in some inaccessible place in the woods. In any case, take care that the spot where they are buried will not stand out because of recently dug-up earth. Cover it with a pile of stones, logs, ashes, or whatever. As for all the military booty, such as uniforms, helmets, belts, and so forth, either burn it or bury it in the same type of place where you bury the bodies. Take this precaution because otherwise another band of robbers will be sure to dig in the freshly moved earth, naturally hoping to find their money or valuables. But when they uncover instead the corpses of their comrades and their belongings, they will be sure to turn on you and burn down the village."

J. PLANAT DE LA FAYE

Letter from Moscow

September 30, 1812

On September 14, 1812, the French army occupied the Russian capital, Moscow. Napoleon expected the czar to sue for peace, but the Russians refused to negotiate. To make matters worse, the city began to burn soon after the French arrived. Most of the buildings Napoleon was counting on to house his troops were destroyed. The following letter from a French officer, J. Planat de la Faye, describes the chaotic situation in the city.

For the past two months, our existence has been extraordinary; we live by pillaging and marauding; the inhabitants leave their cities and villages at our approach and flee into the woods with their animals and provisions; we send our servants, with some soldiers, to besiege them and take their food. We make our own bread, slaughter our own cows, slit the throats of our own sheep; each is his own butcher, baker, cook; this is how we live. . . . Our unfortunate servants must forage two or three leagues from the main routes at the risk of being taken by Cossacks or assassinated by peasants. We are all dirty, tattered, and barefoot, and not a single tailor, shoemaker, or washerwoman. Can you believe that a population of 320,000 souls has disappeared before us! . . .

They say the Russian government burnt its beautiful capital to deprive us of resources we might have found there. I don't know; but our soldiers certainly helped it along. Imagine drunken soldiers with lit candles, torches, matches ransacking wooden houses; that was Moscow the day after our arrival. Fanned by a violent wind, the fire lasted three days. One has never seen such a terrible, frustrating sight.

M. Chaulanges, A. G. Manry, and R. Sève, *Textes historiques, 1799–1815: L'époque de Napoléon* (Paris: Delagrave, 1960), 161–62.

PHILIPPE-PAUL DE SÉGUR

Crossing the Beresina

1825

With the Russians stubbornly refusing to capitulate and with food running out, his soldiers suffering from exposure, and the Russian winter fast approaching, Napoleon decided to abandon Moscow. The retreat became a nightmare, with pillage-laden soldiers freezing by the roadside in arctic temperatures. Discipline began to break down, and entire army units dissolved into masses of panicked individuals trying to save themselves. A scene of extreme chaos occurred at the crossing of the Beresina River, spanned by only two bridges that the entire army had to cross with Russian troops in hot pursuit. The following description of this nightmarish episode is an eyewitness account from the memoirs of General Philippe-Paul de Ségur (1780–1873).

The situation of the 9th Corps [the rear guard] was all the more critical as a weak and narrow bridge was its only means of retreat; moreover, access to it was blocked with baggage and stragglers. As combat intensified, their fear increased the disorder. At first they were frightened by the first sounds of serious battle, then by the sight of the returning wounded, and finally, by Russian batteries . . . whose shells began to fall on the confused mass. . . .

This immense multitude, piled up on the riverbank, pell-mell with horses and carts, formed a horrible jam. Toward the middle of the day, the first enemy shots fell in the midst of this chaos and unleashed universal despair.

As in all extreme situations, true characters were revealed; there were both shameful and sublime actions. Some, enraged and determined, cut themselves a path with sabers. Others carved an even crueler passage for their vehicles, driving them pitilessly through and crushing the helpless crowd. . . . Still others, seized by a disgusting

Philippe-Paul, comte de Ségur, *Histoire de Napoléon et de la Grande Armée pendant l'année 1812*, vol. 2 (Paris: Baudouin frères, 1825), 341–45.

fear, wept, begged, and succumbed, terror draining their strength. Some, especially the sick and wounded, moved aside and sat down hopelessly, staring at the snow that would soon be their tomb.

Many of those in the front of the desperate mob had missed the bridge and tried to climb its trestles; but most were pushed back into the river. There were women among the floating ice with children in their arms, raising them higher and higher as they sank. Even when submerged, their stiff arms still held them up.

Amidst the horrible disorder, the artillery bridge broke. The column crossing it tried vainly to retreat. But the crush of men behind them, unaware of the accident, ignoring the cries of those in front, pushed on and forced them into the abyss, where they in turn were cast.

Then everybody rushed toward the other bridge. A multitude of big caissons, heavy vehicles, and artillery pieces flowed toward it from all sides. . . . Rapidly carried toward the mass of men by the steep and uneven grade, they crushed the unfortunates . . . and then crashed into each other and flipped over violently, killing all around them. . . .

These waves of miserable people rolled in, one on top of the other. All that was heard were cries of pain and rage. In this frightful mêlée, men who had fallen down and were being suffocated grasped tooth and nail at the legs of their companions still afoot. These, however, pushed them mercilessly away, as if they were enemies. . . .

The lucky ones reached the bridge, but only by walking over heaps of fallen, half-smothered injured men, women, and children. They thought themselves saved when they arrived at that narrow passage; but each moment a fallen horse, a broken or missing plank, stopped their progress.

On the other bank, the bridge led to a bog where many horses and carts had gotten stuck, hindering and slowing their flight. Then, in this desperate column crowded on this sole path to safety, an infernal struggle broke out, in which the weakest and poorly placed were cast into the river by the strongest. Without a second glance, these, carried away by their self-preservation instinct, pressed on furiously, ignoring the cries of rage and despair of their companions or leaders, whom they were sacrificing. . . .

72

ERNST MORITZ ARNDT

The German Fatherland

1813

During the French retreat from Russia, the Prussian corps attached to the Grand Army switched sides. Profoundly humiliated by their crushing defeat by Napoleon in 1806–1807, the Prussians had ever since seethed with ill-concealed anger at the French. The same could also be said for many inhabitants of other German states. The defection of the Prussian corps and the destruction of Napoleon's army in Russia brought German feelings into the open. A sense of German nationhood, shaped in no small measure around a core of hatred for the French, began to emerge, encouraged by philosophers, writers, and even the Prussian government. One of the most strident voices calling upon the German nation to rise up and annihilate the French was Ernst Moritz Arndt (1769–1860). His folk song, "The German Fatherland," typifies the spirit of the new German literary nationalism.

What is the German's fatherland?
Is it Prussia? Swabia?
Is it where the grape flowers by the Rhine?
Is it where the seagull soars over the Belt Straits?
Oh no! no! no!
His fatherland must be bigger.

What is the German's fatherland?
Is it Bavaria? The Steiermark?
Is it where the Marsen cow stretches its limbs?

From http://gutenberg.spiegel.de/arndt/gedichte. Translation by Claudia Liebeskind.

Is it where the Markish man works iron?
Oh no! no! no!
His fatherland must be bigger.

What is the German's fatherland?
Is it Pomerania? Westphalia?
Is it where the dune sand blows?
Is it where the Danube loudly flows?
Oh no! no! no!
His fatherland must be bigger.

What is the German's fatherland?
Tell me, what is this great land?
Is it Swiss land? The Tyrol?
That land and people, I like well.
But no! no! no!
His fatherland must be bigger.

What is the German's fatherland?
Tell me, what is this great land?
Certainly it must be Austria,
Rich in honors and victories?
Oh no! no! no!
His fatherland must be bigger.

What is the German's fatherland
Tell me, what is this great land?
As far as the German tongue is heard,
And God in heaven sings German songs.
That shall it be!
That, brave German, call yours.

That is the German's fatherland,
Where oaths are sworn with a firm handshake,
Where loyalty sparkles in the eye,
And love sits warmly in the heart—
That it shall be
That, brave German, call yours.

That is the German's fatherland,
Where fury exterminates foreign trash,

Where every Frenchman is called enemy,
Where every German is called friend—
That shall it be!
All Germany shall it be!

It shall be all Germany!
Oh God in heaven watch over us,
And give us true German courage,
So we love it faithfully and well.
That shall it be!
All Germany shall it be!

73

Proclamation of Kalisch
March 23, 1813

The Prussian monarchy recognized the power of nationalism and sought to draw upon it in the fight against Napoleon. Yet it realized that to unfurl the banner of German nationalism was to play with fire. Not only did nationalism conjure up frightening visions of social upheaval, revolution, and democracy, but it also threatened to give rise to a new entity—Germany—that could overshadow Prussia and thwart Prussian interests. The Prussian monarchy therefore proceeded cautiously, trying to mobilize Germans through nationalistic appeals while at the same time trying to limit their destabilizing potential. The Proclamation of Kalisch (March 23, 1813), issued to the German people when Russian troops began to enter Germany, offers an example of how the Prussian monarchy sought to ride the tiger of nationalism.

Proclamation to the Germans!
    His Majesty the Czar of Russia and His Majesty the King of Prussia announce to the Princes and peoples of Germany the return of free-

Dokumente zur Deutschen Verfassungsgeschichte, ed. Ernst Rudolf Huber, vol. 1 (Stuttgart: W. Kohlhammer, 1960), 72–73. Translation by Claudia Liebeskind.

dom and independence. Their sole aim is to help recover this stolen, but inalienable, birthright of the peoples and to protect and guarantee the rebirth of a venerable empire. This grand goal . . . alone directs the advance of their armies.

Under the eyes of their monarchs, the armies . . . hope to accomplish for the whole world, and irrevocably for Germany, what they so honorably began: to throw off the shameful yoke. Full of enthusiasm they come. Their motto is: honor and freedom! Let every German worthy of the name quickly and forcefully join them; let everybody — Prince, noble, or common man — join the liberation plans of Prussia and Russia with heart and mind, property, blood, body, and life. . . .

And so [Their Majesties] demand faithful cooperation, especially from every German Prince, and they presume they will find among them no traitors to the German cause. . . .

The Confederation of the Rhine, the treacherous shackle with which the sower of division enchained stricken Germany, . . . can be tolerated no longer because it is the result of foreign pressure and tool of foreign influence.

Moreover, Their Majesties are fulfilling a long-cherished and general wish of the people . . . by declaring that the dissolution of this confederation is their firmest intention.

With this [proclamation], we also announce the relationship the Emperor of Russia will have with reborn Germany and its constitution. Because they want to annihilate foreign influence, this [relationship] will necessarily be limited to protecting the task [of constitution-making] which is the sole responsibility of the peoples and Princes of Germany. The more the [constitution] respects the essential character of the German people, the more rejuvenated, vital, and unified will Germany again figure among the European peoples.

74

ANTOINE-CLAIRE THIBAUDEAU

The First Restoration

1913

After a brilliant but doomed campaign to defend France, Napoleon abdicated on April 6, 1814. Close on the heels of the victorious allied armies came the royal retinue of Louis XVIII. The restoration of the Bourbon monarchy in France after a twenty-five-year hiatus elicited a wide range of reactions. In the following excerpt from his memoirs, Antoine-Claire Thibaudeau offers his judgment on France's response to the Bourbon restoration.

Generally, the men of the Revolution and Empire were full of consternation; but, to the shame of humanity and of restorations which warp character and make hypocrites, many . . . tried to keep their positions or obtain equivalent ones. It got to the point that, if the Bourbons had wanted, there would have been almost no change. . . . Adhesions, submissions, abounded; leading dignitaries, grand officers, marshals, high functionaries gave the example; everybody else followed them. They did not only flatter the Bourbons, they cravenly insulted the Emperor. They were the privileged, salaried, titled nation. The other nation, the true one, more numerous, initially dumbstruck, regarded this utterly new spectacle with cold curiosity. . . . The popular masses' noble attitude was particularly remarkable at the entry of Louis XVIII. . . . An immense people was afoot, cold, sad, silent, abandoning calmness only occasionally to mock the grotesque costumes of these returning ghosts. . . . The marshals and generals of the King's escort shamefully rode under the damning weight of their rapid conversion.

Antoine-Claire Thibaudeau, *Mémoires* (Paris: Plon-Nourit, 1913), 399.

Glum and menacing, the Imperial Guard detachments closing the march seemed to be attending the burial of national glory rather than the triumph of the Bourbons. The people understood and applauded. To the serious, impartial observer, this royal entry gave rise to serious reflection.

75

EMMANUEL-AUGUSTE DE LAS CASES

Account of a Conversation between Benjamin Constant and Napoleon

1815

After his abdication, Napoleon was exiled to Elba, where he quickly tired of ruling that pocket kingdom. Informed that the government of Louis XVIII was deeply unpopular and that the allies were falling out with one another over the reorganization of Europe, Napoleon decided to return to France. Accompanied by a handful of stalwarts, he landed on the Mediterranean coast on March 1, 1815, and marched northward toward Paris. The troops sent to capture him defected to their former emperor, and Louis XVIII fled. Now that Napoleon was back in power, his most pressing concern was how to mobilize the nation to face the expected allied onslaught. This task was a political one, and Napoleon faced difficult choices. In the following document, Napoleon weighs his options in a conversation with the liberal political writer Benjamin Constant.

The nation has had twelve years' respite from political agitation and, for one year, from war. After this double dose of rest, it needs activity. It wants, or thinks it wants, a tribune and assemblies. It did not always want them. It threw itself at my feet when I arrived in the government.

Emmanuel-Auguste, comte de Las Cases, *Mémoires de Napoléon 1ᵉʳ* (Mémorial de Sainte-Hélène), vol. 5 (Paris: Cocuaud, n.d.), 76–79.

You, who were in the opposition, should remember. Where was your support, your force? Nowhere. I could have taken more authority than I did. . . . Today, all has changed. A weak government . . . has [accustomed the nation] to distrusting and contesting authority. Taste for constitutions, debates, harangues, seems to have returned. . . . Nonetheless, make no mistake: only the minority wants them. The people, or rather the multitude, want only me. You have not seen this multitude following my steps, leaping from mountain heights, calling me, seeking me, saluting me. From Cannes to Paris, I did not conquer, I administered! . . . I am not only the Emperor of soldiers, I am also Emperor of the peasants, the plebeians of France. . . . Thus, despite the past, the people return to me. There is sympathy between us. It is not so with the privileged. The nobility served me; it crowded into my antechambers. There is no position it did not solicit, demand, accept. I had Montmorencys, Noailles, Rohans, Beauvais, Mortemarts. . . . With the people, it is different: the popular fiber resonates with my own. I emerged from the ranks of the people; my voice touches them. Look at these conscripts, these peasants' sons; I did not flatter them, I treated them sternly; still they surrounded me and cried "Long Live the Emperor!"

They and I are of the same nature. They see me as their support, their savior against the nobles. . . . I have but to make a sign, or even look away, and the nobles will be massacred in the provinces. . . .

But I don't want to be king of a peasant revolt. If constitutional government is possible, in good time! . . . I wanted the empire of the world, and to take it, I needed boundless power. To govern just France, perhaps a constitution is better. . . . I wanted world empire, and who would not have wanted it in my place? The world invited me to rule it. Sovereigns and subjects threw themselves under my scepter. I rarely met resistance in France; but I encountered more of it in certain obscure Frenchmen . . . than in all these kings who are today so proud to no longer have a man of the people as equal. . . .

Political debate, free elections, responsible ministers, freedom of the press, I want all that . . . above all, freedom of the press; to stifle it is absurd. I am convinced of it. . . .

I am a man of the people; if the people want liberty, I will give it. I have recognized their sovereignty; I must listen to their desires, their whims. I never oppressed for pleasure. I had great plans: destiny decided otherwise. I am no longer a conqueror; that I can no longer be. I know what is possible and what is not. I have only one mission now, to raise up France and give her an appropriate government. . . . I do not hate liberty. I brushed it aside when it blocked my way; but I understand it, I was nourished on it. . . . Moreover, the work of 15 years has been destroyed; it cannot recommence. It would take 20 years and 2 million men. . . . I want peace and will only obtain it through victories. I don't want to give you false hopes; I drop hints that there are negotiations, but there are none. I foresee a difficult struggle, a long war. To wage it, the nation must support me; but in return, I believe, it will demand liberty. It will have it. . . . One is not the same at 45 as at 30. The repose of a constitutional king might suit me. It will surely be better for my son.

76

ANTOINE-CLAIRE THIBAUDEAU

The Hundred Days

1913

In this excerpt from his memoirs, Antoine-Claire Thibaudeau offers another view of Napoleon after his return from Elba.

He was not the same. Struck by lightning, he bore the mark. France had also changed. In passing, the royal restoration had reawakened love of liberty in some; it had paid others for their defection. . . . How could the Empire rely on marshals, generals, ministers, senators, notables of all sorts who, whether by egoism or fatalism, had sullied themselves with two defections in less than a year? The sincere Bonapartists were divided. Some cried to the Emperor while raising him up: "We are yours but with conditions: No more despotism! Liberty! Institutions! Guarantees!" The Emperor had to make himself liberal, in spite of himself. . . . Torn between the demands of circumstance and his nature and habits, he was weakened and no longer himself.

Antoine-Claire Thibaudeau, *Mémoires* (Paris: Plon-Nourit, 1913), 459–60.

For these reasons, I would have preferred that Napoleon had presented himself not as Emperor, but as the avenging arm of revolutionized France, exercising dictatorship until the nation, having reconquered its independence by arms and negotiations, constituted its own government. . . . No Chambers, discussions, babbling, but action, action, and still more action. Everything for the war. Make the French people an army and France a fortress. Unfortunately it was very difficult for the Emperor to accept being just a dictator, and a revolutionary one at that. He would have had to leave at home the rotten and worn out instruments of Empire, civilian and military, who had cravenly defected to the Bourbons, and replace them with new, young men, with fortunes to make, able to inspire the people and army. By restoring himself Emperor, fate also required that he restore his former cortege of dignitaries, ministers, councilors of State, marshals, gentlemen, chamberlains, most of whom were doubtful friends, discredited in public opinion, and little inclined to sacrifice themselves for him and the fatherland. . . . The whole imperial reorganization strongly resembled . . . a temporary building constructed with old material.

9

The Aftermath

White Terror, Bourbon Repression

77

CHARLES-ESPRIT MARIE DE LA BOURDONNAYE

Speech to the Legislature
Calling for Royalist Repression

November 11, 1815

After Napoleon's defeat at Waterloo and second abdication, a wave of political violence known as the White Terror swept southern France as opponents of the revolutionary and Bonapartist regimes settled scores with old enemies. As they began their second restoration, the Bourbons were feeling far less merciful than they had in 1814 but were nevertheless concerned that the violence was spinning out of control. To reassert Bourbon authority, they resolved to institutionalize the repression under government supervision. In the following excerpt from a speech he delivered to the legislature, a royalist deputy, Count Charles-Esprit Marie de la Bourdonnaye (1753–1840), elaborates upon this policy.

Archives Parlementaires, series II, vol. 15, 216–17.

To assuage the fears of the multitude, an amnesty is necessary. This amnesty must be grand, generous, irrevocable [but] . . . it can only attain the grandeur necessary to distinguish it from weakness, by excluding those shameless conspirators, those dangerous men who, throughout the Revolution, were prominent in its ranks, exploited it for personal profit, and built their fortune on public calamities. It must exclude those generals, those corps commanders who, traitors to their fatherland, perjurers of their oaths, gave the signal for defection and toppled the throne they were called to defend. . . .

For too long, these artisans of our disasters have hid behind their numerous accomplices and thus escaped their well-deserved punishment. . . .

To halt their criminal plots, we need chains, executioners, torture; death, only death can frighten their accomplices and end their plots. You will note in the history of our Revolution, that rebellion was most frequent under the most moderate governments. Under the Convention's rule and tyrant's iron scepter, however, the perilous effort against tyranny attracted few . . . because men who seem full of love of the public good, who ostentatiously scoff at death under moderate governments which never inflict it, prudently hide when swift justice is placed in the firm hand of an inexorable judge. . . .

Thus, only by inspiring a healthy terror in the soul of rebels can we forestall their guilty projects. Only by cutting off their leaders' heads . . . can we isolate and reduce to its real force this minority which, for 25 years, multiplies its power by uniting its resources and coordinating its efforts. . . .

It was this criminal association that toppled the throne in 1792, organized the Terror in 1793, gave power to five incapable Directors, and then reclaimed it to place on the tyrant's head. It is [this association] which, falling with him, raised him up again last March. Carried along with his fall, it seeks to seize power again and place it on an even more guilty head.

78

Charge Sheet against Suspected Bonapartists

January 3, 1816

Bonapartists and former revolutionaries were not all cowed. In late 1815 they rioted in Montpellier to protest the visit of the Duke d'Angoulême (1775–1844), who had led resistance to Napoleon's return in the south of the country and had encouraged the White Terror. The rising failed, but it induced Bourbon police to arrest hundreds of people on political charges. The following document, a charge sheet drawn up on January 3, 1816, just days after the riot, gives a sense of how the Bourbon authorities construed the crime of "Bonapartism."

Roquier (soldier): said of His Royal Highness the Duke d'Angoulême: "Is that monkey coming? I don't give a damn about our rulers. . . ."

Roche (merchant): repeatedly stated that Bonaparte would soon return. . . .

Etienne (no profession given): wore a blue and white cockade with red thread.

Balp (landowner): said the government is like a bucket going up and down, that having changed 10 times in 19 years, it might well change a dozen more times. . . .

Barban (deserter): cried "Long Live the Emperor" in a billiard hall and insulted the King.

Dejean (ex-soldier): said the triumphal arch erected at Meze for the visit of His Royal Highness the Duke d'Angoulême should be his gallows.

The Quatrefages brothers (court record-keeper): illicit nocturnal meetings at odd hours in their house. . . .

Bertrand (surgeon, intern at the hospital): [found in possession of] a mysterious letter full of effervescences and four other documents, all contrary to Bourbon government and favorable to the usurper.

Carra (wife of Cavanon) and her brother: said the mail of November 26 had not arrived because the Parisians were revolting against the Bourbons. . . .

Archives Départementales de l'Hérault, 1 M 875.

Bouchoni (no profession): limitless attachment to the usurper's government; participated actively in the unfortunate events that occurred in Montpellier on June 27 and July 2, and signed an innkeeper's register under a false name.

Pau: under an arrest warrant for the disastrous events of Montpellier. . . .

Campan (special commissioner of the usurper): held secret nocturnal meetings, criminal correspondence, and attempts or plots to overthrow the royal government. . . .

Vivier (ex-mayor of Pignans) and son: abuse of power and embezzlement . . . during the interregnum; moreover, denounced by public rumor.

Favier (second-lieutenant in the Sete customs house) and Fleuran (sergeant in the Angoulême regiment): seditious speech against the government. . . .

Guruoalsac (half-pay officer): peddling seditious writings in suspicious meetings, abuse, vexation, and excesses against citizens.

Fleuri (wife of Clos): cried "Long Live the Emperor" and "To the Devil with all royalists, may the King burn in hell with them."

79

PREFECT OF THE HÉRAULT

Letter to His Subprefects

December 23, 1815

The Montpellier rioting was a direct expression of opposition to the Bourbons. A more typical way of showing dissatisfaction was by acquiring Napoleonic mementoes — tricolor flags, pictures, statuettes, songbooks — to cherish in private. These could be purchased throughout France, even in remote villages, from the thousands of peddlers who crisscrossed the country. The following document, a letter from the prefect of the Hérault instructing his subordinates to recruit peddlers as spies, shows both the

Archives Départementales de l'Hérault, 1 M 872.

intensity of Bourbon police efforts against, and the widespread persistence of, popular Bonapartism.

His Excellency, the Minister of General Police, has called my attention to the peddlers, sellers of trinkets, books, almanacs, and songs ... who criss-cross France, reaching even the smallest hamlets and most isolated dwellings. He notes that all too often ill will and factionalism use these men as agents of their lies and intriguing, and that henceforth the administration must make them work for legitimate authority.

His Excellency thinks we can use these different kinds of petty merchants to achieve this goal, and that we ought to have them register ... and obtain a passbook. ... You will ... use them to spread useful truths and combat harmful errors. The villager listens to traveling merchants like oracles and is especially inclined to believe them because of their similar dress and language.

There are two ways of getting them to work toward our ends: fear and hope. They must understand that you follow their doings diligently and will punish them if they abuse your confidence, but will reward them if they faithfully execute your orders. Well-chosen examples of severity and liberality will soon convince them of it. I will give you the means to reward them, but these are to be granted only to those worthy of your confidence. They ought to be directed mainly toward those communes where bad spirit reigns; they will report on what they have seen and heard, and we will thus be in a position to strike more surely where we must.

The Specter of Napoleon in the Atlantic World

80

DUKE DE RICHELIEU

Letters to the Marquis d'Osmond

1816–1818

Just as Bourbon authorities were worried about Napoleon's continuing influence within France, they were also concerned about his possible reappearance on the international scene. Their greatest fear was that he would escape from the island-prison of Saint Helena and place himself in a position to do new mischief. The following excerpts from the correspondence of the Bourbon foreign minister, the Duke de Richelieu (1766–1822), to the French ambassador in London seem almost paranoid. Yet to dismiss them as such is perhaps to overlook the enormous prestige Napoleon still enjoyed and the great influence he could exert.

JULY 5, 1816

The attempt to rescue Bonaparte still worries me. . . . Orders sent from Europe [to St. Helena] for tighter surveillance will arrive too late and, while I cannot foresee any success for him in France, it is nonetheless true that an escape would be, wherever he ended up, an endless source of trouble for our poor country. In sum, it is sad to see this man in the hands of a people who, by changing [their government], could initiate events that could return him to the world stage.

SEPTEMBER 12, 1816

Regarding the slave trade, I [enclose] a letter I just received from Monsieur Hyde de Neuville [French ambassador to the United States]. . . . It deserves attention because it suggests a link between

Lettres du duc de Richelieu au marquis d'Osmond, 1816–1818, ed. Sébastien Charlety (Paris: Gallimard, 1939), 46–189.

the expeditions of American pirates to the African coast and a possible attempt against St. Helena.... Draw the full attention of the English government to this object.... We must always keep our telescopes focused on that rock in the Atlantic. It is easy to say he has lost all credibility in Europe; I would like to believe it. But I would not be very comfortable if we had to put it to the test; the last thing in the world I would like would be to learn he was free.

SEPTEMBER 8, 1817

When combining all the indications I have gleaned, I find it hard to believe there is no project afoot to overthrow the established order in France and bring back Buonaparte [*sic*]. I am fully aware that it seems impossible to free him without the cooperation of the English government. But, given the prestige still surrounding him and his influence over those near him, must we not fear that he can weave some plot at St. Helena to aid his escape? I admit that this thought, that I have often had, has constantly troubled me.

FEBRUARY 5, 1818

There is no doubt that the agitators and malcontents of all countries look to St. Helena, certainly not from love of the man imprisoned there, but because they view his reappearance on the scene as a means of upsetting and destroying the established order. They reserve for themselves the right to fight him once he has helped them triumph. It is thus extremely important to be sure that his escape or rescue is impossible, and it is only from England that we can hope for that assurance. Therefore, do not lose a single occasion to remind the ministers of the importance of the charge with which they are entrusted and for which they are responsible to the whole of Europe. It should not be difficult for you to convince your Russian, Austrian, Prussian, and Spanish colleagues to join you and speak with one voice on this object.

MAY 25, 1818

The English government favors as much as it can the insurrection of the Spanish provinces. That policy, which presently invigorates the factories of Great Britain, seems quite narrow and miserable compared to the great concerns we have to deal with.

These reflections . . . bring me back, in spite of myself, to St. Helena and the possibility of an escape. Sometimes I get the idea that [the English] would not be very upset by it, because it would certainly destroy all credit in France and all hope of improvement. I stifle this thought, but I am sure that if such a misfortune occurred, everyone would form this conjecture and hold the English government responsible for an event which it is fully capable of preventing if it so desired. I never believed in the possibility of a frontal attack [on St. Helena by the partisans of Napoleon], but I admit that I greatly fear an escape, certainly not favored by the English government, but in which it would be the dupe of a man more canny than us all.

81

JOSE GARCIA DE LEON Y PIZARRO

Circular Letter to the Cabinets of Europe

1817

The fear that Napoleon might escape from Saint Helena and again wreak havoc on the world was shared by other conservative statesmen of Europe. The Spanish government was particularly concerned that Napoleon might seek in the revolt of its American colonies a new field for his devilish talents and unquenched ambition. In this diplomatic note from the Spanish cabinet to the other governments of Europe, foreign minister Jose Garcia de Leon y Pizarro (1770–1835) raised the specter of the Napoleonic appropriation of the Latin American independence movement to achieve Spanish political objectives.

The European malcontents and criminals who have sought refuge in the U.S. have leagued with Bonaparte and seek to continue in the New World his plans of ambition, usurpation, and disorder. They hope to establish in these dominions the reign of usurpation, fortunately thwarted in Europe by the efficiency and union of the sovereigns and their peoples' efforts. This new object . . . opens a new perspective for the consideration of the European cabinets and, casting a frightening

Jose Garcia de Leon y Pizarro, *Memorias*, ed. Alvaro Alonso-Castrillo, vol. 1 (Madrid: Revista de Occidente, 1964), 280–85.

light on the affairs of America, threatens their most immediate and sensitive interests, disappoints their deepest hopes, and menaces the destruction of ... the European system, established at such great cost. ...

Such plans are intimately related to the fate of Napoleon himself. ... The allies cannot disregard the new aspect these circumstances give to the whole matter of the revolution in America. ... The emergence of an independent America under republican governments would make pacification a direct, public matter, and an intimately European cause. The illusion of liberalism, impossible in those regions, would be dispelled. It is easy to prove that European superiority and trade can only find advantage in the reasoned submission and union of the overseas provinces under a legitimate monarch. How much more pressing this interest when one considers that America has become the theater of organized subversion, usurpation, and domination under the hateful name of a family that has destroyed thrones and public happiness everywhere in Europe! The cause of America is not only the cause of a false and impossible liberty; it is the cause of Napoleon's domination ... which [will now] be reinforced with the abundant physical resources of a fertile country. It would have been in vain that Europe had liberated herself from this frightful domestic enemy; soon, she will be attacked even more terribly by the same enemy. The continental system, ridiculous because it is impossible in Europe, will soon acquire a fatal reality. ...

The American revolution is the European revolution; for it to be completely so, all that is lacking is for the Bonaparte family to take a personal part in it. Already this evil combination has been realized. The vexations exercised by the insurgent pirates against world trade, increasing every day, demand armed intervention. Only a confederation of the great powers, a sincere and strong manifestation of their intentions, and a decision to display their power if needed will end the rule of the factious, encourage the loyal, and consolidate the political structure, built with so many sacrifices and on whose durability human happiness depends.

Popular Bonapartism

82

PIERRE-JEAN DE BÉRANGER
The Old Banner
1820

Despite the increasingly hierarchical, even courtly mutation the regime had experienced after 1804, Bonapartism after 1815 was primarily a popular movement. Although he had stripped them of liberty and sent hundreds of thousands of young men to their deaths in his wars, Napoleon was remembered fondly, even passionately, by large numbers of French people of all walks of life. Bonapartist sentiment was nourished by a number of sources: personal recollections, images, statuettes, flags, and literature. One of the most powerful forms of Bonapartist expression was song and poetry. The following poem is by Pierre-Jean de Béranger (1780–1857), the Bonapartist bard whose numerous works, particularly after 1815, helped forge the Napoleonic legend.

With my few trusty comrades in glory of yore,
I see me surrounded in fancy once more:
Our proud recollections 'tis vain to control,
The wine renders back all their glow to my soul:
Our high deeds in arms from the starry Past leap,
In my poor ruined hut our Old Banner I keep.
Ah! When from its colors of pride shall I shake
The tarnishing dust, and bid heroes awake?

'Neath my pallet of straw I have hid it away,
Where, poor, maimed, and weary, my old head I lay,
That Banner which, ever to Victory true,

Pierre-Jean de Béranger, *Béranger's Poems*, trans. W. Falconer (Philadelphia: J. B. Lippincott, 1888), 81–82.

From battle to battle for twenty years flew;
O'er Europe's wide kingdoms unrivalled it shone,
Encircled with laurels and flowers all its own.
Ah! when from its colors of pride shall I shake
The tarnishing dust, and bid heroes awake?

This Banner repaid to our war-battered host
And to France, glory-crowned, all the blood that it cost:
Our sons with its lance upon Liberty's breast
Sported free, and its ne'er-beaten eagle caress'd:
Let it prove to the tyrants who crush us with wrongs
How much of true fame to the people belongs.
Ah! when from its colors of pride shall I shake
The tarnishing dust, and bid heroes awake?

All low in the dust its bold eagle now bleeds,
Fatigued with its flight and its far famous deeds;
The old Gaulish Cock to his colors bestow
The thunder it also can hurl on the foe:
France, forgetting her sorrows, great, glorious, and free!
Shall pour forth her blessings again upon thee.
Ah! when from its colors of pride shall I shake
The tarnishing dust, and bid heroes awake?

83

FRENCH CONSUL IN NEW ORLEANS

Dispatch to the French Foreign Minister
May 1817

Popular Bonapartism's appeal was not limited to France. It existed throughout the Atlantic world, but perhaps to no greater degree than in the city of New Orleans. The former capital of French Louisiana was home to a bustling population of Franco-Spanish creoles, refugees from

Archives des Affaires Etrangères, Correspondance Politique, Etats-Unis, 74.

*Saint-Domingue, a transient maritime community, recent French eco-
nomic immigrants, and even political exiles driven from France by the
Bourbons. This population, moreover, supported the Mexican independence movement against royalist Spain and burned hot with anglopho-
bia (the city had been attacked by the English in 1815). These elements
combined to produce strong Bonapartist sentiment in the city. Public
manifestations in favor of Napoleon, some of which were violent, were a
frequent occurrence in New Orleans during the 1810s and 1820s. The
following dispatch from the French consul there describes an incident
that occurred on May 4, 1817.*

A play entitled "The Day of the Three Emperors, or the Eve of the
Battle of Austerlitz," most likely produced for the circumstance when
it first appeared in Paris, was performed last Sunday, May 4th, in the
city's principal theater.

In this performance, the flag and cockade of the usurper were
prominently displayed to the repeated acclamations of "Long Live the
Emperor! Long Live Napoleon!" of an immense crowd . . . including
many individuals with tricolor cockades on their hats. Between acts,
the famous airs of various periods of our revolution were enthusiastically called for and sung. Finally, to complete this scene—which was
as ridiculous (when one notes that it occurred in a foreign republic) as
it was indecent and even outrageous (when one considers that this
republic enjoys peaceful and friendly relations with France)—couplets
insulting the King, royal family, and all the classes of individuals which
today form His Majesty's government, were carried to the front of the
stage, handed to the mayor (who was present), given by him to an
actor, and sung to the "bravos!" of the mass of spectators, who added
their voices to the actor's at each refrain.

The next morning, having heard an exact and detailed account of
everything that happened in that revolutionary farce, I immediately
went to the house of Monsieur the General de la Villeré, governor of
the state, and expressed to him my surprise at such a gratuitous insult
directed almost under his very eyes against the august head of a
friendly nation of which I had the honor to be the agent.

84

BERNARD-ADOLPHE GRANIER DE CASSAGNAC

On Popular Bonapartism
and Louis-Napoleon's Rise to Power

1857

Bonapartism remained a potent political force in France itself, helping Napoleon's nephew, Louis Napoleon, found a new empire in 1852. Below, the fervent Bonapartist journalist Bernard-Adolphe Granier de Cassagnac (1806–1880) offers his explanation for the persistent appeal of Bonapartism.

It was in June, under the weight of dark apprehensions generated by the approach of the inevitable clash of demagogy and socialism, that the name Louis-Napoleon suddenly illuminated the shadows of the future. The star appeared simultaneously to city workers, peasants, and shepherds. . . .

The Empire had not fallen, like the Old Regime or Restoration, under the weight of public opinion. In 1789 and 1830, the people had rejoiced; in 1815, the people had cried. The memory of Louis XVI and Charles X were relegated to history; that of Napoleon, still alive and radiant, fills the world, respected by foreigners and beloved of the French.

A million soldiers, debris of the armies of Italy, Egypt, Germany, Russia, spread across the cities, villages, and countryside, bringing to even the poorest house the immortal legend of the Consulate and Empire. There, while the veteran told the new generation about battles won, the father about order re-established, and the grandmother about churches reopened and cleansed. Innumerable and unknown rhapsodies spread through the workshops and fields the naïve shreds of the finest epics; and the matinal worker, like the straggling cowhand, sang in all the idioms of France verses in which great glory and misfortune alternated: Austerlitz and St. Helena.

A. Granier de Cassagnac, *Histoire de la chute du roi Louis-Philippe, de la République de 1848, et du rétablissement de l'Empire* (Paris: Plon, 1857), 11–15.

The lettered muse joined the rustic muse, and France rendered in glory to its poets the songs devoted to its Emperor. Some were eloquent and sublime; others were simple and touching, faithful expressions of the regrets and reverence for France:

> We will speak of his glory
> For many years under the thatch
> In fifty years the humble roof
> Will know other story[1]

And while the poets, dramatic authors, historians evoked the venerated memory of the Emperor in their odes, chronicles, and tragedies, his features—reproduced by bronze, marble, cloth, and popular imagery—crowned monuments, decorated museums, galleries, books, and went to take their place at the laborer's bedside, between the evergreen or blessed laurel and the family's patron saint.

A regime which penetrates so deeply a nation's ideas and sentiments is not dead; it was only sleeping. What was needed to awaken it and have it rise again? A revolution, a commotion, an event that would place France's destiny in the hands of the people.

Superficial minds who thought that the Empire was but a man might have thought it permanently put to sleep beneath the willows of Saint-Helena. Attentive and incisive minds, those who knew that the Empire was the Revolution of 89 become government, believed it was as immortal as the Revolution itself.

The political classes who, in 1815 and 1830, had appropriated power could, by moderation, wisdom, and patriotism, prolong the duration of the oligarchic regime; but the day when a general upheaval would unleash the free intervention of the people, the Empire would be restored.

---

[1] From Béranger, *Les souvenirs du peuple.* [Original footnote.]

Return of the Ashes

85

VICTOR HUGO

Napoleon's Reburial in France
1840

In July 1830 a new revolution overthrew the Bourbon regime. A monarchy headed by Louis-Philippe, Duke d'Orléans (1773–1850), took its place. In 1840 the July Monarchy returned Napoleon's remains to France from Saint Helena, where he had died in 1821. The celebrated writer Victor Hugo (1802–1885) witnessed the return of the ashes and later visited Napoleon's burial tomb. These experiences, described in the following excerpts from his diary, gave him the opportunity to reflect broadly on the Napoleonic phenomenon.

Suddenly cannon fire echoed from three different points on the horizon. This simultaneous, triple noise enclosed the ear in a formidable and superb triangle. Distant drums beat in the fields.

The Emperor's coach appeared.

Veiled until that instant, the sun suddenly burst through. The effect was prodigious.

Far off, in the mist and sun, against the rust-grey background of the trees of the Champs-Elysées, through the huge white statues that resembled phantoms, we could see a kind of golden mountain slowly move. We could not yet distinguish anything but a sort of luminosity that made the entire surface of the coach shine with stars and flashes. An immense murmur enveloped this apparition.

One could say the coach drew with it the acclamation of the entire city just as a torch leaves behind a smoky trail.

When it turned onto the avenue of the Esplanade, it halted briefly

Victor Hugo, *Journal, 1830–1848*, ed. Henri Guillemin (Paris: Gallimard, 1954; repr., Westport, Conn: Greenwood Press, 1970), 47–49 and 66–67.

in front of a statue. . . . I later learned that it was the statue of Marshal Ney.

It was half past one when the funeral coach appeared.

The cortege resumed its course.

The coach advanced slowly. We began to make out its form.

First, were the horses of the marshals and generals serving as imperial pallbearers.

Then came 86 non-commissioned officers, all decorated with the Legion of Honor, carrying the banners of the 86 departments. Nothing could be more beautiful than this phalanx, above which waved a forest of flags. . . .

Finally came a white horse covered from head to toe in purple crepe, accompanied by a sky-blue, silver-embroidered chamberlain and led by two footmen in gold-trimmed green. It was the Emperor's livery. A shiver went through the crowd: "It is Napoleon's war horse!" Almost everyone was convinced of it. But even if the horse had served the Emperor only two years, it would have been 30 years old, remarkably long-lived for a horse. . . .

When it arrived before me, something stopped it. The coach halted. It remained motionless for several minutes between the statues of Joan of Arc and Charles V.

I could look at it closely. The overall effect was not without grandeur. It was an enormous mass, entirely golden, whose tiers rose like a pyramid above its four large gilded wheels. Beneath the purple, bee-strewn crepe which covered it from top to bottom, one could see some pretty details: the stunned eagles of the base, the 14 Victories of the summit bearing the simulacrum of a coffin on a golden table. The real coffin was invisible. It was in a compartment in the base, which diminished the emotion.

That was the coach's most serious fault. It hid what we wanted to see, what France demanded, what the people awaited, what all eyes were seeking, Napoleon's coffin.

The false sarcophagus was covered with the Emperor's insignias: crown, sword, scepter, and mantle. Between the Victories on high and eagles below, one could see (in spite of the gilding, which had already half peeled off) the suture lines of pine planks. Another defect. The gold was only gold in appearance. Pine and cardboard, that was the reality. I would have wanted for the Emperor's coach a sincere magnificence. . . .

I arrived at the threshold of St. Jerome Chapel.

A grand archivolt with a tall portiere of fairly cheap purple cloth *printed* with Greek frets and golden palm leaves; at the top of the portiere, the imperial escutcheon in painted wood; to the left, two bundles of tricolor flags topped by eagles, which resembled chickens touched up for the occasion; old veterans decorated with the Legion of Honor, pikes in hand; the silent and respectful crowd entering under the vault; 8 or 10 steps inside, an iron gate painted bronze; on the gate ... lion heads, golden "N"s which looked like pasted-on tinsel, the imperial coat of arms, the hand of justice and the scepter crowned by a figurine of Charlemagne seated, crown on head and globe in hand; above the gate, the interior of the chapel, which was indescribably august, formidable, and arresting, a lighted lamp, a huge golden eagle with wings spread wide, whose breast was shining with the reflection of the funeral lamp and whose wings caught a flash of sunlight; below the eagle, under a vast and breathtaking bouquet of enemy flags, the coffin, whose ebony feet and bronze rings could be seen; on the coffin, the grand imperial crown similar to Charlemagne's, the diadem of golden laurel leaves similar to Caesar's, the pall of purple velour festooned with bees; in front of the coffin, on a credenza, the hat from St. Helena and sword from Eylau; on the wall, to the right of the coffin, in the middle of a silvered shield the word *Wagram*; to the left, in the center of another shield, the word *Austerlitz*; all around, on the wall, funeral hangings of purple velour embroidered with bees and eagles; above, at the top of the vault, above the lamp, the eagle, the crown, the sword, and the coffin, a fresco and, in that fresco, the angel of judgment blowing his trumpet upon sleeping St. Jerome,—that is what I saw in a flash, that is what one minute burned into my memory for all my lifetime.

The wide-brimmed hat, little-used, decorated with a black braid, from which hung a tiny tricolor cockade, was placed on the sword, whose engraved golden grip was turned toward the chapel entrance, whose point was toward the coffin.

There was cheapness and tawdriness mixed with this grandeur. What made it so was the printed (not embroidered) purple cloth, the cardboard painted to look like stone, the hollow iron painted to look like bronze, the wooden escutcheon, those "N"s made from thin metal strips, the canvas stele painted to look like granite, the chicken-like eagles. What made it grand was the place, the man, the reality, the sword, the hat, the eagle, the soldiers, the people, the ebony coffin, the ray of sun.

The crowd stood there as if present before an altar where God was visible. But after leaving the chapel, ... they stopped off at the canteen. Such is the nature of the crowd.

Last Words

86

EMMANUEL-AUGUSTE DE LAS CASES

Napoleon on Napoleon

undated

Napoleon spent the last eight years of his life as a prisoner of the British on the remote South Atlantic island of Saint Helena. One of his principal occupations was recounting his life to various stalwarts and companions who accompanied him into exile or visited him periodically on the island. Four of these — General Henri-Gatien Bertrand (1773–1844), General Gaspard Gourgaud (1783–1852), Court Chamberlain Emmanuel de Las Cases, and General Charles de Montholon (1783–1853) — recorded his sayings and later published them, under various titles, as the memoirs of Napoleon. While these are valuable sources, they must be read critically, for Napoleon was speaking to his memorialists with a definite purpose in mind: to shape his own legacy for posterity. With the following excerpt from Las Cases's memoir, we leave Napoleon the last word.

I sealed the chasm of anarchy and ordered the chaos. I purified the Revolution, ennobled the people, and reinforced kings. I encouraged striving, rewarded merit of all sorts, and pushed back the limits of glory! What can one blame me for, what is there that a historian cannot defend? My intentions? But they were fundamentally pure. My despotism? But dictatorship was an urgent necessity. Will they say I hindered liberty? But permissiveness, anarchy, and serious disorders were knocking at the door. Will they accuse me of having loved war too much? But I was always under attack. To have aspired to universal monarchy? But it was only the fortuitous consequences of circumstance [and] our enemies themselves who gradually led me there.

Emmanuel-Auguste, comte de Las Cases, *Mémoires de Napoléon 1ᵉʳ* (Mémorial de Sainte-Hélène), vol. 7 (Paris: Cocuaud, n.d.), 54–55.

Finally, my ambition? Ah, doubtless I had much, but of perhaps the grandest and most elevated sort ever! That of establishing, consecrating the rule of reason and the full exercise and enjoyment of all human faculties! And here perhaps the historian will find himself reduced to regretting that this ambition was not accomplished and fulfilled!

A Chronology of Napoleon and His Times
(1769–1821)

1769   *August 15*: Napoleon is born in Ajaccio, Corsica.

1778–
1785   *December 1778–October 1785*: Napoleon attends military school in France.

1789   *July 14*: Mobs storm the Bastille; the French Revolution begins.

1793   *June*: The Bonaparte family flees Corsica.

       September–December: Napoleon commands the artillery at Toulon.

1794   *July 27*: On 9 Thermidor, Robespierre is overthrown, and the Terror ends.

       August: Napoleon is briefly imprisoned but is subsequently cleared of all charges.

1795   *October 5*: Napoleon helps suppress the Vendémiaire uprising.

1796   *March 9*: Napoleon marries Josephine Beauharnais.

1796–
1797   *April 1796–April 1797*: Napoleon conducts the first Italian campaign, during which France defeats Piedmont and Austria.

1797   *September 3–4*: The coup d'état of 18 Fructidor takes place.

       October 17: The Treaty of Campo Formio is signed with Austria.

1798–
1799   *May 1798–August 1799*: Napoleon leads the Egyptian campaign.

1799   *October 9*: Napoleon arrives back in France.

       November 9–10: The coup d'état of 18 Brumaire takes place.

       December 13: The Consulate is established.

1800–
1801   *January 1800–February 1801*: Napoleon promotes policies of reconciliation and order, including the pacification of the Vendée, amnesty for emigrés, and special tribunals.

1800   *May–July*: Napoleon conducts the second Italian campaign; at the Battle of Marengo, France defeats Austria.

1801   *February 9*: The Treaty of Lunéville is signed with Austria.

July 16: The Concordat with the papacy is signed.

1801–
1803   *December 1801–November 1803*: Napoleon sends an expedition to Haiti.

1802   *March 25*: The Treaty of Amiens is signed with Britain.

May: *Lycées* and the Legion of Honor are created; slavery is restored.

August 2: The position of Consul-for-Life is created.

1803   *May 3*: Napoleon sells Louisiana to the United States.

May: The Peace of Amiens collapses.

1803–
1804   *May 1803–March 1804*: The Civil Code is debated and approved.

1804   *May 18*: Napoleon is proclaimed emperor.

1805   *May 26*: Napoleon is crowned king of Italy.

July–August: The Third Coalition (Britain, Russia, Austria) is formed.

October 20: At the Battle of Ulm, France defeats Austria.

October 21: At the Battle of Trafalgar, Britain defeats a Franco-Spanish fleet.

December 2: At the Battle of Austerlitz, France defeats Austria and Russia, forcing an Austrian surrender on December 25.

1806   *March–July*: The satellite kingdoms of Naples and Holland are formed.

July–August: The Confederation of the Rhine is created; the Holy Roman Empire is dissolved.

October 14: At the Battles of Jena and Auerstadt, France defeats Prussia.

November 21: The Berlin Decree establishes the continental blockade.

1807   *February 8*: France fights Russia at the Battle of Eylau.

June 14: At the Battle of Friedland, France defeats Russia.

July 7 and 9: The Treaties of Tilsit are signed with Russia and Prussia.

July–August: The Grand Duchy of Warsaw and the kingdom of Westphalia are created.

October: French troops enter Spain.

November–December: The Milan Decrees are issued to reinforce the continental blockade.

1808   *March 1*: The imperial nobility is created.

May 2: The Madrid rising signals the beginning of anti-French resistance.

June 6: Joseph is named king of Spain.

1809   *April–October*: France fights war against Austria.

May 21–22: At the Battle of Aspern-Essling, Austria defeats France.

July 5–6: France defeats Austria at the Battle of Wagram.

October 14: The Treaty of Schönbrunn is signed with Austria.

December 15: Napoleon divorces Josephine.

1810   *April 2*: Napoleon marries Marie-Louise of Austria.

July: Napoleon annexes Holland.

December: Napoleon annexes parts of northern Germany.

1811   *March 20*: A son is born to Marie-Louise and Napoleon.

1812   *January*: Napoleon annexes Catalonia.

June 4: The United States declares war on Britain (War of 1812).

June: Napoleon begins the Russian campaign.

September 7: At the Battle of Borodino, France defeats Russia.

September 14: Napoleon enters Moscow.

October 18: Napoleon begins retreat from Russia.

1813   *March*: Prussia declares war on France.

August 12: Austria declares war on France.

October 16–19: At the Battle of Leipzig, Austria, Prussia, and Russia defeat France.

December: The allies cross the Rhine and begin the invasion of France.

1814   *January–March*: The campaign of France is waged.

April 6: Napoleon abdicates; the Bourbons are restored.

December 4: The United States and Britain sign the Treaty of Ghent, ending the War of 1812.

1814–
1815   *April 1814–February 1815*: Napoleon is in exile on Elba.

1815   *March 1*: Napoleon returns to France.

March–June: Napoleon reigns once more during the Hundred Days.

June 18: At the Battle of Waterloo, Britain and Prussia defeat France.

June 22: Napoleon abdicates; the Bourbons are restored.

July 26: Napoleon sets sail for Saint Helena.

1821 *May 5*: Napoleon dies on Saint Helena.

Questions for Consideration

1. How did the different elements in Napoleon's post-Brumaire political settlement interact with and reinforce one another? Why did different groups (revolutionaries, emigrés, the church, among others) accept this settlement?

2. What roles did Napoleon intend for the institution of the family to play in his social and political projects?

3. What was the Napoleonic understanding of merit?

4. Did Napoleonic creations like the Legion of Honor, the imperial dynasty, and the imperial nobility preserve or betray the revolutionary legacy?

5. What was the international impact of the establishment of the empire in 1804? Of the imperial nobility in 1807?

6. Napoleon was a master of propaganda. How did the self-image he sought to project change during the course of his rule and after 1815?

7. What was the impact of the Napoleonic wars on the people of Europe?

8. In judging his impact on Europe, is Napoleon best characterized as a liberator or an exploiter?

9. Many historians have described Napoleon as a dictator. Is this the best description of his rule?

10. What was the basis of Napoleon's legitimacy? How did it change over the course of his reign and after?

Selected Bibliography

REFERENCE WORKS

Chandler, David. *Dictionary of the Napoleonic Wars.* New York: Macmillan, 1979.
Emsley, Clive. *The Longman Companion to Napoleonic Europe.* London and New York: Longman, 1993.
Tulard, Jean. *Dictionnaire Napoléon.* Paris: Fayard, 1987.

PRINTED PRIMARY WORKS

Las Cases, Emmanuel. *Memoirs of the Life, Exile, and Conversations of the Emperor Napoleon.* 4 vols. London: Richard Bentley, 1836.

BIOGRAPHIES

Englund, Stephen. *Napoleon: A Political Life.* Cambridge, Mass.: Harvard University Press, 2004.
Thompson, J. M. *Napoleon Bonaparte.* Oxford: Blackwell, 1988.

GENERAL

Ellis, Geoffrey. *The Napoleonic Empire.* New York: Palgrave-Macmillan, 2003.
Lyons, Martin. *Napoleon Bonaparte and the Legacy of the French Revolution.* New York: St. Martin's, 1994.
Tulard, Jean. *Napoleon: The Myth of the Saviour.* Trans. Theresa Waugh. London: Methuen, 1985.

NAPOLEONIC FRANCE

Bergeron, Louis. *France under Napoleon.* Princeton, N.J.: Princeton University Press, 1981.
Crook, Malcolm. *Napoleon Comes to Power: Democracy and Dictatorship in Revolutionary France, 1795–1804.* Cardiff: University of Wales Press, 1998.
Forrest, Alan. *Conscripts and Deserters: The Army and French Society during the Revolution and Empire.* Oxford: Oxford University Press, 1989.

Sutherland, D. M. G. *France, 1789–1815: Revolution and Counter Revolution.* New York and London: Oxford University Press, 1986.

Woloch, Isser. *Napoleon and His Collaborators: The Making of a Dictatorship.* New York and London: W. W. Norton, 2001.

———. *The New Regime: Transformations of the French Civic Order, 1789–1820s.* New York and London: W. W. Norton, 1994.

NAPOLEON AND EUROPE

Broers, Michael. *Europe under Napoleon, 1799–1815.* London: Arnold, 1996.

Connelly, Owen. *Napoleon's Satellite Kingdoms.* New York: Free Press, 1965.

Dwyer, Philip, ed. *Napoleon and Europe.* London: Pearson, 2001.

Grab, Alexander. *Napoleon and the Transformation of Europe.* London: Palgrave-Macmillan, 2003.

Schroeder, Paul. *The Transformation of European Politics, 1763–1848.* Oxford: Oxford University Press, 1994.

Woolf, Stuart. *Napoleon and the Integration of Europe.* London and New York: Routledge, 1991.

NAPOLEON AND THE ATLANTIC

Dubois, Laurent. *Avengers of the New World: The Story of the Haitian Revolution.* Cambridge, Mass.: Belknap, 2004.

Geggus, David, ed. *The Impact of the Haitian Revolution in the Atlantic World.* Columbia: University of South Carolina Press, 2001.

Stone, Bailey. *The Genesis of the French Revolution: A Global-Historical Interpretation.* Cambridge: Cambridge University Press, 1994.

NAPOLEON AND ART

O'Brien, David. *After the Revolution: A-J Gros, Painting, and Propaganda under Napoleon.* University Park: Pennsylvania State University Press, 2005.

Prendergast, Christopher. *Napoleon and History Painting: Antoine-Jean Gros's "La Bataille d'Eylau."* Oxford: Oxford University Press, 1997.

Wilson-Smith, Timothy. *Napoleon and His Artists.* London: Constable, 1996.

WAR

Bell, David A. *The First Total War: Napoleon's Europe and the Birth of Warfare As We Know It.* Boston: Houghton Mifflin, 2007.

Blanning, T. C. W. *The French Revolutionary Wars, 1787–1802.* London and New York: Arnold, 1996.

Connelly, Owen. *Blundering to Glory: Napoleon's Military Campaigns.* Wilmington, Del.: Scholarly Resources, 1999.

Esdaile, Charles. *The Wars of Napoleon.* London and New York: Longman, 1995.

Forrest, Alan. *Napoleon's Men: The Soldiers of the Revolution and Empire.* London and New York: Hambledon and London, 2002.

Rothenberg, Gunther. *The Art of Warfare in the Age of Napoleon.* Bloomington: Indiana University Press, 1978.

END OF EMPIRE

Alexander, R. S. *Bonapartism and Revolutionary Tradition in France: The Fédérés of 1815.* Cambridge: Cambridge University Press, 1991.

Bertier de Savigny, Gilbert. *The Bourbon Restoration.* Trans. L. Case. Philadelphia: University of Pennsylvania Press, 1967.

Lewis, Gwynne, *The Second Vendée: The Continuity of Counter-Revolution in the Department of the Gard, 1789–1815.* Oxford: Clarendon, 1978.

Mackenzie, Norman. *The Escape from Elba: The Fall and Flight of Napoleon, 1814–1815.* New York: Oxford University Press, 1985.

LEGACY

Broers, Michael. *Europe after Napoleon: Revolution, Reaction, and Romanticism, 1814–1848.* Manchester: Manchester University Press, 1996.

Hazareesingh, Sudhir. *The Legend of Napoleon.* London: Granta, 2004.

Laven, David, and Lucy Rial, eds. *Napoleon's Legacy: Problems of Government in Restoration Europe.* Oxford and New York: Berg, 2000.

Ménager, Bernard. *Les Napoléon du people.* Paris: Aubier, 1988.

Acknowledgments (continued from p. iv)

Document 3   "Historical, Political, and Military Notes on the Army of Italy."
Courrier de l'armée d'Italie, no. 48, 2 Brumaire VII/October 23, 1797, 205–6.
Courtesy of David A. Bell.

Document 12   "Letter on Brigandage." Archives de la Guerre, B^{13} 119, letter of Challamel, director of the jury of the arrondissement of Largentière (24
Pluviôse VIII). Courtesy of Howard Brown.

Document 37   Paret, Peter; *On War.* © 1976 Princeton University Press,
2004 renewed Princeton University Press. Reprinted by permission of Princeton University Press.

Document 60   "Confidential Instructions to General Leclerc." *Lettres du
Général Leclerc, commandant en chef de l'armée de Saint-Domingue en 1802,*
ed. Paul Roussier (Paris: Ernest Leroux, 1937), 269–72. Courtesy of Laurent
Dubois and John Garrigus.

Index